ILTS 135 Foreign Language: Spanish
Teacher Certification Exam

By: Sharon Wynne, M.S.

XAMonline, INC.
Boston

Copyright © 2013 XAMonline, Inc.
All rights reserved. No part of the material protected by this copyright notice may be reproduced or utilized in any form or by any means, electronic or mechanical, including photocopying, recording or by any information storage and retrievable system, without written permission from the copyright holder.

To obtain permission(s) to use the material from this work for any purpose including workshops or seminars, please submit a written request to:

> XAMonline, Inc.
> 25 First Street, Suite 106
> Cambridge, MA 02141
> Toll Free 1-800-301-4647
> Email: info@xamonline.com
> Web www.xamonline.com

Library of Congress Cataloging-in-Publication Data

Wynne, Sharon A.
    Foreign Language: Spanish 135: Teacher Certification / Sharon A. Wynne. -2nd ed.
    ISBN 978-1-58197-988-6
    1. Foreign Language: Spanish 135.   2. Study Guides.   3. ILTS
    4. Teachers' Certification & Licensure.   5. Careers

Disclaimer:
The opinions expressed in this publication are the sole works of XAMonline and were created independently from the Pearson Corporation, National Education Association, Educational Testing Service, or any State Department of Education, National Evaluation Systems or other testing affiliates.

Between the time of publication and printing, state specific standards as well as testing formats and website information may change that is not included in part or in whole within this product. Sample test questions are developed by XAMonline and reflect similar content as on real tests; however, they are not former tests. XAMonline assembles content that aligns with state standards but makes no claims nor guarantees teacher candidates a passing score. Numerical scores are determined by testing companies such as NES or ETS and then are compared with individual state standards. A passing score varies from state to state.

Printed in the United States of America

ILTS: Foreign Language: Spanish 135
ISBN: 978-1-58197-988-6

TEACHER CERTIFICATION EXAM

About the Subject Assessments

ILTS™: Subject Assessment in the Spanish examination

Purpose: The assessments are designed to test the knowledge and competencies of prospective secondary level teachers. The question bank from which the assessment is drawn is undergoing constant revision. As a result, your test may include questions that will not count towards your score.

Test Version: There is one version of subject assessment for Spanish examination in Illinois. The test emphasizes comprehension in speaking, writing, listening and reading Spanish, as well as knowledge of the languages structure, culture, appropriate vocabulary and pedagogy. The Spanish examination guide is based on a typical knowledge level of persons who have completed a *bachelor's degree program* in Spanish.

Time Allowance and Format: You will have 5 hours to complete the test. The exam consists of 100 multiple-choice questions; one written constructed-response assignment; one oral constructed-response assignment which will be recorded on audio-tape.

Additional Information about the ICTS Assessments: The ILTS™ series subject assessments are developed by the *National Evaluation Systems*. They provide additional information on the ICTS series assessments, including registration, preparation and testing procedures, study materials such as topical guides that are about 35 pages of information including approximately 15 additional sample questions.

FOREIGN LANGUAGE: SPANISH

TEACHER CERTIFICATION EXAM

TABLE OF CONTENTS

Page Numbers

SUBAREA I—LISTENING COMPREHENSION 1

0001 Demonstrate an understanding of oral communication in Spanish 1

0002 Derive essential information from oral messages in real-life situations 1

0003 Infer meaning from oral communications 2

SUBAREA II—READING COMPREHENSION 3

0004 Demonstrate an understanding of written passages in Spanish 3

0005 Demonstrate an understanding of the content of a variety of authentic written materials 4

0006 Apply skills of inference and interpretation to a variety of authentic written materials 7

SUBAREA III—LANGUAGE STRUCTURES AND LANGUAGE ACQUISITION .. 13

0007 Transform sentences or passages in context according to given instructions 13

0008 Identify correct words or phrases needed to complete sentences accurately 13

0009 Demonstrate the ability to identify correct academic usage 14

0010 Understand processes involved in second- and heritage-language acquisition 40

SUBAREA IV—CULTURAL KNOWLEDGE 42

0011 Demonstrate familiarity with manners, customs, and ranges of cultural expression in various Spanish-speaking communities 42

0012 Demonstrate familiarity with the arts (e.g., music, dance, folk, art, visual art, drama, architecture) and literature of various Spanish-speaking communities 44

0013 Demonstrate familiarity with the history, geography, demographics, and economics of various areas where Spanish is spoken 51

SUBAREA V—WRITTEN EXPRESSION 75

0014 Use Spanish to present in writing information, concepts, and ideas for a variety of purposes to different audiences 75

SUBAREA VI—ORAL EXPRESSION 76

0015 In response to a prompt, effectively communicate an oral message in Spanish that includes a range of vocabulary, idiomatic expressions, complex language structures, and sociolinguistic appropriateness 76

Bibliography 77

Tables - Grammar and Maps 79

Practice Test 91

Answer Key 114

TEACHER CERTIFICATION EXAM

Great Study and Testing Tips!

What to study in order to prepare for the subject assessments is the focus of this study guide but equally important is *how* you study.

You can increase your chances of truly mastering the information by taking some simple, but effective steps.

Study Tips:

1. Some foods aid the learning process. Foods such as milk, nuts, seeds, rice, and oats help your study efforts by releasing natural memory enhancers called CCKs (*cholecystokinin*) composed of *tryptophan*, *choline*, and *phenylalanine*. All of these chemicals enhance the neurotransmitters associated with memory. Before studying, try a light, protein-rich meal of eggs, turkey, and fish. All of these foods release the memory enhancing chemicals. The better the connections, the more you comprehend.

Likewise, before you take a test, stick to a light snack of energy boosting and relaxing foods. A glass of milk, a piece of fruit, or some peanuts all release various memory-boosting chemicals and help you to relax and focus on the subject at hand.

2. Learn to take great notes. A by-product of our modern culture is that we have grown accustomed to getting our information in short doses (i.e. TV news sound bites or USA Today style newspaper articles.)

Consequently, we've subconsciously trained ourselves to assimilate information better in neat little packages. If your notes are scrawled all over the paper, it fragments the flow of the information. Strive for clarity. Newspapers use a standard format to achieve clarity. Your notes can be much clearer through use of proper formatting. A very effective format is called *"Cornell Method."*

> Take a sheet of loose-leaf lined notebook paper and draw a line all the way down the paper about 1-2" from the left-hand edge.
>
> Draw another line across the width of the paper about 1-2" up from the bottom. Repeat this process on the reverse side of the page.

Look at the highly effective result. You have ample room for notes, a left hand margin for special emphasis items or inserting supplementary data from the textbook, a large area at the bottom for a brief summary, and a little rectangular space for just about anything you want.

3. Get the concept then the details. Too often we focus on the details and don't gather an understanding of the concept. However, if you simply memorize only dates, places, or names, you may well miss the whole point of the subject.

A key way to understand things is to put them in your own words. If you are working from a textbook, automatically summarize each paragraph in your mind. If you are outlining text, don't simply copy the author's words.

Rephrase them in your own words. You remember your own thoughts and words much better than someone else's, and subconsciously tend to associate the important details to the core concepts.

4. Ask Why? Pull apart written material paragraph by paragraph and don't forget the captions under the illustrations.

Example: If the heading is "Stream Erosion", flip it around to read "Why do streams erode?" Then answer the questions.

If you train your mind to think in a series of questions and answers, not only will you learn more, but it also helps to lessen the test anxiety because you are used to answering questions.

5. Read for reinforcement and future needs. Even if you only have 10 minutes, put your notes or a book in your hand. Your mind is similar to a computer; you have to input data in order to have it processed. *By reading, you are creating the neural connections for future retrieval.* The more times you read something, the more you reinforce the learning of ideas.

Even if you don't fully understand something on the first pass, *your mind stores much of the material for later recall.*

6. Relax to learn so go into exile. Our bodies respond to an inner clock called biorhythms. Burning the midnight oil works well for some people, but not everyone.

If possible, set aside a particular place to study that is free of distractions. Shut off the television, cell phone, pager and exile your friends and family during your study period.

If you really are bothered by silence, try background music. Light classical music at a low volume has been shown to aid in concentration over other types. Music that evokes pleasant emotions without lyrics are highly suggested. Try just about anything by Mozart. It relaxes you.

FOREIGN LANGUAGE: SPANISH

7. Use arrows not highlighters. At best, it's difficult to read a page full of yellow, pink, blue, and green streaks. Try staring at a neon sign for a while and you'll soon see that the horde of colors obscure the message.

A quick note, a brief dash of color, an underline, and an arrow pointing to a particular passage is much clearer than a horde of highlighted words.

8. Budget your study time. Although you shouldn't ignore any of the material, *allocate your available study time in the same ratio that topics may appear on the test.*

TEACHER CERTIFICATION EXAM

Testing Tips:

1. Get smart, play dumb. Don't read anything into the question. Don't make an assumption that the test writer is looking for something else than what is asked. Stick to the question as written and don't read extra things into it.

2. Read the question and all the choices *twice* before answering the question. You may miss something by not carefully reading, and then re-reading both the question and the answers.

If you really don't have a clue as to the right answer, leave it blank on the first time through. Go on to the other questions, as they may provide a clue as to how to answer the skipped questions.

If later on, you still can't answer the skipped ones . . . **Guess.** The only penalty for guessing is that you *might* get it wrong. Only one thing is certain; if you don't put anything down, you will get it wrong!

3. Turn the question into a statement. Look at the way the questions are worded. The syntax of the question usually provides a clue. Does it seem more familiar as a statement rather than as a question? Does it sound strange?

By turning a question into a statement, you may be able to spot if an answer sounds right, and it may also trigger memories of material you have read.

4. Look for hidden clues. It's actually very difficult to compose multiple-foil (choice) questions without giving away part of the answer in the options presented.

In most multiple-choice questions you can often readily eliminate one or two of the potential answers. This leaves you with only two real possibilities and automatically your odds go to Fifty-Fifty for very little work.

5. Trust your instincts. For every fact that you have read, you subconsciously retain something of that knowledge. On questions that you aren't really certain about, go with your basic instincts. **Your first impression on how to answer a question is usually correct.**

6. Mark your answers directly on the test booklet. Don't bother trying to fill in the optical scan sheet on the first pass through the test.

Just be very careful not to miss-mark your answers when you eventually transcribe them to the scan sheet.

7. Watch the clock! You have a set amount of time to answer the questions. Don't get bogged down trying to answer a single question at the expense of 10 questions you can more readily answer.

FOREIGN LANGUAGE: SPANISH

TEACHER CERTIFICATION EXAM

SUBAREA I—LISTENING COMPREHENSION

0001 Demonstrate an understanding of oral communication in Spanish.

See sample test questions #21-25.

> Claudio: ¿Hola, cómo has estado?
>
> Don Fintesco: Perfecto, ¿Qué necesitas?
>
> Claudio: Pues te cuento, tengo mucha plata, mis negocios van bien y ahora te voy a proponer una nueva empresa en la cual tu me puedes ayudar. Resulta que en mis viajes conocí una princesa sueca y ella me hablo de su amor de las esmeraldas y la falta de aquéllas en su colección personal. Naturalmente le ofrecí mi ayuda.
>
> Don Fintesco: Se pone interesante tu cuento. ¿Cuanto crees que va ella a pagar por la piedra de sus sueños?
>
> Claudio: No es para soñar, sino para vivir, mi apreciado amigo. Ella llega este viernes y tu tarea es de darme a mí no antes del jueves en la media noche, una piedra de quince quilates.
>
> Don Fintesco: ¿Cómo que estás loco? ¿Adónde voy a encontrar una piedra así en tres días, adentro de mi zapato?
>
> Claudio: No me importan los detalles, tráela el jueves y te daré cuarenta porciento de lo que gane en la venta. ¡Hasta entonces, amigo!

0002 Derive essential information from oral messages in real-life situations.

Para usar Grow! Shampoo:

> "Simplemente moje su cabello, dé un masaje en todo su pelo, y déjeselo por 3 minutos y luego enjuague. Puede dar una segunda pasada, si usted gusta, pero Grow! hace el trabajo en una. A su vez, Grow! contiene ingredientes delicados que le permitén que se use a diario, y así usted no necesita estar alternando de shampoos."

To use Grow! Shampoo:

"Simply wet your hair, massage it onto all your hair and leave for three minutes and then rinse. Can be given a second time over, if you like, but Grow! does the work at once. At the same time, Grow! contains delicate ingredients that permit daily use for you and that way, you don't need to be alternating with other shampoos."

http://www.sucabello.com/instrucciones.htm

0003 Infer meaning from oral communications.

Buenos días señor, estamos llamándolo a usted debido a la razón de su reciente visita a nuestra agencia de viajes, donde mencionó su interés para viajar este fin de semana para la isla Paraíso con un plan que no exigiera un presupuesto demasiado alto para satisfacer sus requerimientos. Con su permiso lo podría enlistar en nuestro plan de costos rebajados y así rápidamente entregar sus boleta para su próxima destinación.

* * *

¿Me puedes hacer el favor de explicar, amigo mío, qué hace un hombre al despertarse y cómo se viste cuando va salir para trabajar? Primero se baña; después se pone la ropa interior; la camisa con cuello y la corbata; los calcetines; el pantalón y un par de zapatos; el chaleco y el saco. Come desayuno y antes de salir para la calle, se pone el sombrero y la chaqueta.

* * *

La cocina en una casa de huéspedes es muy importante. A las siete en la mañana se sirve desayuno. ¿Qué es él desayuno? Es la primera comida del día. Consiste generalmente de tostadas; huevos pasados por agua; frutas (naranjas o toronjas),;café con leche y tal vez un cereal. Para almorzar se puede tomar una sopa y fideos,(Pasta) o arroz con carne y ensalada. La cena, que consiste en un plato de carne o uno de pescado con legumbres y después una ensalada, se come antes de acostar. Luego, se sirve un postre de fruta, pastel con queso, o torta y dulce. Un café negro sigue de chocolate o leche con galletas.

TEACHER CERTIFICATION EXAM

SUBAREA II—READING COMPREHENSION

0004 Demonstrate an understanding of written passages in Spanish.

See sample test questions #119-125.

I. In the last sentence of the fourth page in the passage what does the coronel's wife mean?

- A. She doesn't want to die suffering.
- B. She wants the lights turned on.
- C. She says that with the lights turned off, she will die.
- D. She doesn't want to die in the fog.

Answer: A

II. What feeling is expressed by the coronel in his closing words in the passage, spoken to his wife?

- A. Hate.
- B. Love.
- C. Abandon.
- D. Envy.

Answer: C

See written example in 747–06.

III. The third time Don Fintesco speaks he uses "Cómo" as an adverb and not a preposition. How does that change the quality of what he is expressing?

- A. He is showing surprise and incredulous disbelief at Claudio's request.
- B. He is addressing Claudio, because he is insane.
- C. He is asking Claudio why he is losing his sanity.
- D. He is disrespecting Claudio.

Answer: A

FOREIGN LANGUAGE: SPANISH

0005 Demonstrate an understanding of the content of a variety of authentic written materials.

En 'Maki Roll' hay sushi y comida japonesa, pero la gracia es comer platos típicos de Corea.

Esta sí no se la sabía. Seguro que no. A menos que haya ido por allá, seguro que un kimchi, una sopa de mandú, un bulgogi o un bibibimbap le suenan a... coreano.

Y no tiene por qué conocerlos. Pero ojo: ya tiene la oportunidad de probar una de las comidas de más intensidad en sus sabores en un menú diseñado para coreanos, pero también para el gusto local. En un pequeño restaurante del norte, Maki Roll, en el que además hay un supermercado de productos orientales bastante completo, está esta sorpresa.

Ahora, la traducción: lo básico que debe saber es que el kimchi está hecho de repollo y es el encurtido picante para acompañar todas las comidas. Que el mandú son empanaditas deliciosas en una sopa. Que la pasta chapche es transparente. Que el bugogi tiene carne y, por supuesto, kimchi. Y que el bibimbap está coronado por un huevo y une a seis verduras con carne de res. ¿La recomendación? Descubrir el lugar. Ah, remate con un té, por supuesto.

From "Llegó la hora de probar lo coreano," April 10 2006. In Eskpe, El Tiempo. Retreived April10, 2006 from:

http://eskpe.eltiempo.terra.com.co/secc_eskpe/rest_eskpe/otrasnoticias/ARTICULO-WEB-NOTA_INTERIOR_ESKPE-2829130.html

               *   *   *

El presidente venezolano, Hugo Chávez, ha amenazado al embajador de EEUU, William Brownfield, con expulsarle del país "si insiste" en provocar situaciones irregulares que involucren "al pueblo venezolano".

"Si usted va a seguir provocando vaya preparando sus maletas porque lo voy a echar de aquí, embajador Brownfield.

Lo voy a echar de Venezuela si sigue provocando al pueblo venezolano, se va a tener que ir de aquí", afirmó Chávez en su programa dominical de Radio y televisión 'Aló, Presidente!'.

Agregó que su Gobierno responderá "igual" si Washington "tomara alguna medida contra Venezuela motivado" por las "provocaciones de Brownfield", al que calificó de "demagogo, ridículo y cínico".

Chávez consideró que Brownfield "provocó" un incidente el viernes pasado cuando grupos oficialistas lanzaron tomates y otro tipo de alimentos y persiguieron con motos la caravana diplomática en un sector del oeste de Caracas.

El representante diplomático, que acudió a una escuela infantil de béisbol para donar guantes, bates y bolas, se presentó en el lugar sin haber anunciado previamente de su presencia a las autoridades venezolanas, argumentó Chávez en su programa de radio y televisión.

Tras sostener que su gobierno "rechaza cualquier agresión" contra diplomáticos o ciudadanos, aseguró que Brownfield actúa de forma "irresponsable" cuando se presenta intempestivamente en lugares donde supuestamente no es bien recibido.

Recalcó que pese a que Brownfield "no coordinó ni con (la) Cancillería ni con la Alcaldía Mayor" de Caracas su visita al barrio de Coche, policías locales acudieron para "protegerlo".

Chávez se quejó además de que el Departamento de Estado de EEUU "amenaza" a Venezuela por el suceso del viernes en vez de "darle instrucciones claras a su embajador, que se ha convertido en un provocador".

"El señor embajador de EEUU está irrespetando la Convención de Viena y entonces después viene el imperio y nos amenaza. "¡Es usted el provocador, señor embajador!", insistió Chávez.

El Departamento de Estado acusó de "complicidad" a las autoridades locales de Caracas por el incidente del viernes y advirtió al embajador venezolano en Washington, Bernardo Alvarez, de que habrá "consecuencias diplomáticas severas" entre ambos países si se produce otro incidente por el estilo.

El canciller venezolano encargado, Alcides Rondón, dijo el sábado que Caracas responderá con "reciprocidad" si la Casa Blanca decide "restringir los desplazamientos" de Alvarez por Estados Unidos.

Rondón señaló que los "excesos inexcusables" del viernes contra Brownfield fueron resultado de una serie de "situaciones bien fortuitas, o bien planificadas", que se habría evitado de haberse coordinado la visita del embajador con las autoridades locales.

Citó además que desde febrero pasado, cuando Caracas expulsó del país por "espía" al agregado militar de EEUU, los agentes venezolanos encargados de la custodia de Brownfield no tienen acceso a la legación diplomática ni a la agenda del embajador.

Las recientes giras y actos públicos de Brownfield en Venezuela han sido truncadas por seguidores de Chávez, que acusa a EEUU de estar detrás de planes desestabilizadores para derrocarlo.

Brownfield ha expresado su preocupación por la falta de seguridad durante sus giras por Venezuela, que ha anunciado que no suspenderá, sin embargo.

Las relaciones diplomáticas entre Venezuela y EEUU están marcadas por constantes acusaciones mutuas, referidas al corte "imperialista e intervencionista" de Washington y a las "intenciones totalitarias" de Chávez, respectivamente.

From "Chávez amenaza con expulsar al embajador de EEUU en Caracas por 'provocador'" April 10, 2006. In elmundo.es, El Mundo. Retrieved April 10, 2006 from:

http://www.elmundo.es/elmundo/2006/04/10/internacional/1144620118.html

0006 Apply skills of inference and interpretation to a variety of authentic written materials.

El coronel... volvió a abrirse paso, sin mirar a nadie, aturdido por los aplausos y los gritos, y salió a la calle con el gallo bajo el brazo.

Todo el pueblo -la gente de abajo- salió a verlo pasar seguido por los niños de la escuela. Un negro gigantesco trepado en una mesa y con una culebra enrollada en el cuello vendía medicinas sin licencia en una esquina de la plaza. De regreso del puerto un grupo numeroso se había detenido a escuchar su pregón.
Pero cuando pasó el coronel con el gallo la atención se desplazó hacia él. Nunca había sido tan largo el camino de su casa.

No se arrepintió. Desde hacía mucho tiempo el pueblo yacía en una especie de sopor, estragado por diez años de historia. Esa tarde -otro viernes sin carta- la gente había despertado. El coronel se acordó de otra época. Se vio a sí mismo con su mujer y su hijo asistiendo bajo el paraguas a un espectáculo que no fue interrumpido a pesar de la lluvia. Se acordó de los dirigentes de su partido, escrupulosamente peinados, abanicándose en el patio de su casa al compás de la música. Revivió casi la dolorosa resonancia del bombo en sus intestinos.

Cruzó por la calle paralela al río, y también allí encontró la tumultuosa muchedumbre de los remotos domingos electorales. Observaban el descargue del circo. Desde el interior de una tienda una mujer gritó algo relacionado con el gallo. Él siguió absorto hasta su casa, todavía oyendo voces dispersas, como si lo persiguieran los desperdicios de la ovación de la gallera.
En la puerta se dirigió a los niños.

-Todos para su casa -dijo-. Al que entre lo saco a correazos.

Puso la tranca y se dirigió directamente a la cocina. Su mujer salió asfixiándose del dormitorio.
-Se lo llevaron a la fuerza -gritó-. Les dije que el gallo no saldría de esta casa mientras yo estuviera viva.

El coronel amarró el gallo al soporte de la hornilla. Cambió el agua al tarro, perseguido por la voz frenética de la mujer.

-Dijeron que se lo llevarían por encima de nuestros cadáveres -dijo-. Dijeron que el gallo no era nuestro, sino de todo el pueblo.

Sólo cuando terminó con el gallo el coronel se enfrentó al rostro trastornado de su mujer. Descubrió sin asombro que no le producía remordimiento ni compasión.

-Hicieron bien -dijo calmadamente. Y luego, registrándose los bolsillos, agregó, con una especie de insondable dulzura-: El gallo no se vende.

Ella lo siguío hasta el dormitorio. Lo sintió completamente humano, pero inasible, como si lo estuviera viendo en la pantalla de un cine.
El coronel extrajo del ropero un rollo de billetes, lo juntó al que tenía en lo bolsillos, contó el total y lo guardó en el ropero.

-Ahí hay veintinueve pesos para devolvérselos a mi compadre Sabas -dijo-. El resto se le paga cuando venga la pensión.

-Y si no viene... -preguntó la mujer.

-Vendrá.

-Pero si no viene...

-Pues entonces no se le paga.

Encontró los zapatos nuevos debajo de la cama. Volvió al armario por la caja de cartón, limpió la suela con un trapo y metió los zapatos en la caja, como los llevó su esposa el domingo en la noche. Ella no se movió.

-Los zapatos se devuelven -dijo el coronel-. Son trece pesos más para mi compadre.

-No los reciben -dijo ella.

Tienen que recibirlos -replicó el coronel-. Sólo me los he puesto dos veces.

-Los turcos no entienden de esas cosas -dijo la mujer.

-Tienen que entender.

-Y si no entienden...

-Pues entonces que no entiendan.

Se acostaron sin comer. El coronel esperó a que su mujer terminara el rosario para apagar la lámpara. Pero no pudo dormir. Oyó las campanas de la censura cinematográfica, y casi en seguida -tres horas después- el toque de queda.
La pedregosa respiración de la mujer se hizo angustiosa con el aire helado de la madrugada. El coronel tenía aún los ojos abiertos cuando ella habló con una voz reposada, conciliatoria.

-Estás despierto.

-Sí.

-Trata de entrar en razón -dijo la mujer-. Habla mañana con mi compadre Sabas.
 -No viene hasta el lunes.
 -Mejor -dijo la mujer-. Así tendrás tres días para recapacitar.
 -No hay nada que recapacitar -dijo el coronel.

El viscoso aire de octubre había sido sustituido por una frescura apacible. El coronel volvió a reconocer a diciembre en el horario de los alcaravanes. Cuando dieron las dos, todavía no había podido dormir. Pero sabía que su mujer también estaba despierta. Trató de cambiar de posición en la hamaca.
 -Estás desvelado -dijo la mujer.
 -Sí.
Ella pensó un momento.
 -No estamos en condiciones de hacer esto -dijo-. Ponte a pensar cuántos son cuatrocientos pesos juntos.
 -Ya falta poco para que venga la pensión -dijo el coronel-.
 -Estás diciendo lo mismo desde hace quince años.
 -Por eso -dijo el coronel-. Ya no puede demorar mucho más.

Ella hizo un silencio. Pero cuando volvió a hablar, al coronel le pareció que el tiempo no había transcurrido.
 -Tengo la impresión de que esa plata no llegará nunca -dijo la mujer.
 -Llegará.
 -Y si no llega...

Él no encontró la voz para responder. Al primer canto del gallo tropezó con la realidad, pero volvió a hundirse en un sueño denso, seguro, sin remordimientos. Cuando despertó, ya el sol estaba alto. Su mujer dormía. El coronel repitió metódicamente, con dos horas de retraso, sus movimientos matinales, y esperó a su esposa para desayunar.

Ella se levantó impenetrable. Se dieron los buenos días y se sentaron a desayunar en silencio. El coronel sorbió una taza de café negro acompañada con un pedazo de queso y un pan de dulce. Pasó toda la mañana en la sastrería. A la una volvió a la casa y encontró a su mujer remendando entre las begonias.
 -Es hora del almuerzo -dijo.
 -No hay almuerzo -dijo la mujer.

Él se encogió de hombros. Trató de tapar los portillos de la cerca del patio para evitar que los niños entraran a la cocina. Cuando regresó al corredor, la mesa estaba servida.

En el curso del almuerzo el coronel comprendió que su esposa se estaba forzando para no llorar. Esa certidumbre lo alarmó. Conocía el carácter de su mujer, naturalmente duro, y endurecido todavía más por cuarenta años de amargura. La muerte de su hijo no le arrancó una lágrima.

Fijó directamente en sus ojos una mirada de reprobación. Ella se mordió los labios, se secó los párpados con la manga y siguió almorzando.
-Eres un desconsiderado -dijo.
El coronel no habló.
-Eres caprichoso, terco y desconsiderado -repitió ella. Cruzó los cubiertos sobre el plato, pero en seguida rectificó supersticiosamente la posición-. Toda una vida comiendo tierra, para que ahora resulte que merezco menos consideración que un gallo.
-Es distinto -dijo el coronel.
-Es lo mismo -replicó la mujer-. Debías darte cuenta de que me estoy muriendo, que esto que tengo no es una enfermedad, sino una agonía.
El coronel no habló hasta cuando no terminó de almorzar.
-Si el doctor me garantiza que vendiendo el gallo se te quita el asma, lo vendo en seguida -dijo-. Pero si no, no.

Esa tarde llevó el gallo a la gallera. De regreso encontró a su esposa al borde de la crisis. Se paseaba a lo largo del corredor, el cabello suelto a la espalda, los brazos abiertos, buscando el aire por encima del silbido de sus pulmones. Allí estuvo hasta la prima noche. Luego se acostó sin dirigirse a su marido.

Masticó oraciones hasta un poco después del toque de queda. Entonces el coronel se dispuso a apagar la lámpara. Pero ella se opuso.

-No quiero morirme en tinieblas -dijo.

El coronel dejó la lámpara en el suelo. Empezaba a sentirse agotado.

Tenía deseos de olvidarse de todo, de dormir de un tirón cuarenta y cuatro días y despertar el veinte de enero a las tres de la tarde, en la gallera y en el momento exacto de soltar el gallo pero se sabía amenazado por la vigilia de la mujer.

-Es la misma historia de siempre -comeñzó ella un momento después-. Nosotros ponemos el hambre para que coman los otros. Es la misma historia desde hace cuarenta años.

El coronel guardó silencio hasta cuando su esposa hizo una pausa para preguntarle si estaba despierto. Él respondió que sí. La mujer continuó en un tono liso, fluyente, implacable.

-Todo el mundo ganará con el gallo, menos nosotros. Somos los únicos que no tenemos ni un centavo para apostar.

-El dueño del gallo tiene derecho a un veinte por ciento.

-También tenías derecho a tu pensión de veterano después de exponer el pellejo en la guerra civil. Ahora todo el mundo tiene su vida asegurada, y tú estás muerto de hambre, completamente solo.

-No estoy solo -dijo el coronel.

Trató de explicar algo, pero lo venció el sueño. Ella siguió hablando sordamente hasta cuando se dio cuenta de que su esposo dormía. Entonces salió del mosquitero y se paseó por la sala en tinieblas. Allí siguió hablando. El coronel la llamó en la madrugada.

Ella apareció en la puerta, espectral, iluminada desde abajo por la lámpara casi extinguida. La apagó antes de entrar al mosquitero. Pero siguió hablando.

-Vamos a hacer una cosa -la interrumpió el coronel.
-Lo único que se puede hacer es vender el gallo -dijo la mujer.
-También se puede vender el reloj.
-No lo compran.
-Mañana trataré de que Álvaro me dé los cuarenta pesos.
-No te los da.
-Entonces se vende el cuadro.

Cuando la mujer volvió a hablar estaba otra vez fuera del mosquitero. El coronel percibió su respiración impregnada de hierbas medicinales.

-No lo compran -dijo.

-Ya veremos -dijo el coronel suavemente, sin un rastro de alteración en la voz-. Ahora duérmete. Si mañana no se puede vender nada, se pensará en otra cosa.

Trató de tener los ojos abiertos, pero lo quebrantó el sueño. Cayó hasta el fondo de una substancia sin tiempo y sin espacio, donde las palabras de su mujer tenían un significado diferente. Pero un instante después se sintió sacudido por el hombro.
-Contéstame.
El coronel no supo si había oído esa palabra antes o después del sueño. Estaba amaneciendo. La ventana se recortaba en la claridad verde del domingo. Pensó que tenía fiebre. Le ardían los ojos y tuvo que hacer un gran esfuerzo para recobrar la lucidez.

-Qué se puede hacer si no se puede vender nada -repitió la mujer.
-Entonces ya será veinte de enero -dijo el coronel, perfectamente consciente-. El veinte por ciento lo pagan esa misma tarde.
-Si el gallo gana -dijo la mujer-. Pero si pierde. No se te ha ocurrido que el gallo puede perder.
-Es un gallo que no puede perder.
-Pero supónte que pierda.
-Todavía faltan cuarenta y cinco días para empezar a pensar en eso -dijo el coronel.
La mujer se desesperó.
-Y mientras tanto qué comemos -preguntó, y agarró al coronel por el cuello de la franela. Lo sacudió con energía-. Dime, qué comemos.
El coronel necesitó setenta y cinco años -los setenta y cinco años de su vida, minuto a minuto- para llegar a ese instante. Se sintió puro, explícito, invencible, en el momento de responder:
-Los Demonios.

From "El coronel no tiene quien le escriba" by Gabriel García Márquez 1958. In Google book search, Google.

Retrieved April 10, 2006 from:

http://books.google.com/books?ie=UTF-8&id=n7V6eF32nOoC&dq=Gabriel+garc%C3%ADa+m%C3%A1rquez+%2Bcoronel&psp=wp&pg=PR4&printsec=3&lpg=PR4&sig=Wp6uzGbQxpwIigSRsfATHnypjFo

TEACHER CERTIFICATION EXAM

SUBAREA III—LANGUAGE STRUCTURES AND LANGUAGE ACQUISITION

0007 Transform sentences or passages in context according to given instructions.

See Sample Test questions #41-47

0008 Identify correct words or phrases needed to complete sentences accurately.

I. Yo te oí. Tú me ____.

    A. ellos

    B. rojo

    C. oyes

    D. avión

Answer: C

II. ¡Oiga! En verdad, quiero que me ____.

    A. oigas

    B. mundo

    C. arroz

    D. llueves

Answer: A

III. En la primera época del año sufrí mucho, pero _____ paro mi sufrimiento.

    A. la mascota se

    B. de pronto

    C. fue un

    D. adonde

Answer: B

TEACHER CERTIFICATION EXAM

0009 Demonstrate the ability to identify correct academic usage.

Spanish punctuation is similar to English, but there are some major differences. They are as follows:

- The comma is used at the end of restrictive relative phrases and is not used before *y*, *e*, *o*, *u* and *ni* in a series.
- Questions have an inverted question mark at the beginning in addition to the one at the end.
- Exclamatory sentences have an inverted exclamation point at the beginning in addition to the one at the end.
- In decimals, Spanish uses a comma where English uses a period.
- Final question marks in Spanish precede the comma or period.

* * *

Accents in Spanish are used to mark a word's stressed syllable –the loud syllable. They are tiny symbols used to identify the correct usage of the word and the pronunciation and punctuation to which it belongs in the sentence. It is placed over the one vowel in the word that is used as accented.

The stressed syllable in Spanish is classified as either "prosódico" (prosodic) or "ortográfico" (orthographic). A prosodic syllable is basically, a syllable with no accent, meaning that the word will project its own innate pronunciation which the reader will understand unaided. Its rules are as follows:

- Words ending in a consonant, excluding "n" or "s", are stressed on the last syllable
- Words ending in any vowel, "n" and "s" have are stressed on the last syllable

Orthographic syllables are pointed out by marking the enunciated syllable with an accent mark –mostly to present a second meaning or to clarify the pronunciation taking exception to the unaccented general rules.

In addition to the classification of stress, Spanish has rules in order to define the resulting accent and stress between two or three adjoined vowels, each within a separate syllable within one word. Vowels are classified as "vocales abiertas tónicas o fuertes" (strong vowels) or "vocales cerradas atónas" (weak vowels) and they are formed into one compound syllable according to the vowels' union and the rule which is imposed.

- Strong vowels (vocales abiertas tónicas) : "a," "e," "o"
- Weak vowels (vocales cerradas atónitas) : "i," "u,"

The rules are as follows:

FOREIGN LANGUAGE: SPANISH

Diphthong:

Two vowels are pronounced as one syllable. It is formed with two adjoining weak vowels; one weak vowel following one strong vowel; one strong vowel following one weak vowel. When "h" lies between both vowels it does not prevent it from being formed.

Tripthong:

Three vowels are pronounced and connected as one syllable. It is formed by a weak vowel, followed by a strong vowel, followed by a weak vowel: this is the only form for the rule.

Hiato:

Is a sequence of two vowels that that are not pronounced within one syllable, but form two consecutive syllables. It is formed with all combinations of weak and strong vowels.

Accents are applied and recognized according to the following rules:

Agudas:

Have a written accent in the last syllable according to its ending in "n" or "s", or any written vowel; but not with any other consonant.

Graves or Llanas:

Have a written accent in the second-to-last syllable when the last syllable ends in "n" or "s"; but not with any other consonant or any vowel.

Esdrújulas:

Have a written accent in the third-to-last syllable with no exceptions.

Sobresdrújulas:

Have a written accent in the fourth-to-last syllable with no exceptions.

Diphtong:

It follows "Aguda," "Grave/Llana," "Esdrújula," "Sobreesdrújula," accent rules. When formed by a weak/weak vowel combination it places the accent on the second vowel. When formed by a strong/weak or weak/strong vowel combination places the accent on the strong vowel.

Triphtong:

It follows "Aguda," "Grave/Llana," "Esdrújula," "Sobreesdrújula," accent rules and accents only the strong vowel.

Hiato:

When formed by weak/weak or strong/strong vowel combination follows "Aguda," "Grave/Llana," "Esdrújula," "Sobreesdrújula," accent rules. When formed by a weak/strong or strong/weak vowel combination always carries an accent on the weak vowel.

Specific Accents:

- Personal Pronouns: "mí," "tú," él,"
- Demonstrative Pronouns: "éste." "ése," "aquél,"
- Interrogative pronouns: "qué," "cuál,"
- "sólo": only if
- "aún": still
- "dé": verb form of "dar"; give
- "sé: verb form of "saber"
- 'más": accented in every form not used as conjunction
- "té": tea
- "sí": affirmative command, third person reflexive pronoun
- "cómo": how
- "ó": or, is used with an accent when comparing two different numerical quantities

TEACHER CERTIFICATION EXAM

Vamos a entrar a mi cuarto.
Verb   Prep.   Verb.   Prep.   Pron.   Noun.

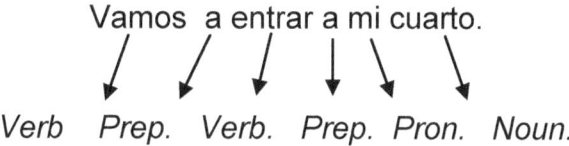

Con él fui a el parque de recreación.
Prep.   Pron.   Verb.   Prep.   Def Art.   Noun.

¿Tú eres mi papa?
Pron.   Verb.   Pron.   Noun.

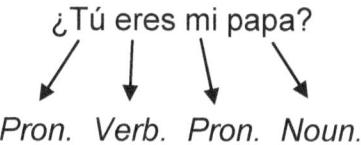

Si fuistes el hombre en el noticiero no me digas.
Prep.   Verb.   Def Art.   Noun   Prep.   Def Art.   Noun.   Adv.   Pron.   Verb.

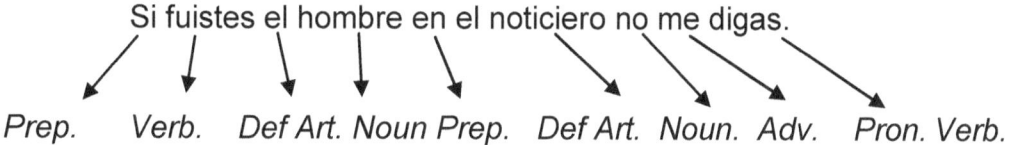

Destruyeron al sol.
Verb.   Prep.   Noun.

El arete brillante se perdió.
Def Art   Noun.   Adj.   Pron.   Adv.

FOREIGN LANGUAGE: SPANISH

Present Indicative

Use of the present indicative tense:

- To refer to the here and now
- To refer to an immediate future
- To refer to an historical past (hace + an expression of time _ que + verb in the present indicative)

Dropping the infinitive ending and adding the following endings form the present indicative of regular verbs:

-ar verbs (-o, -as, -a, -amos, -ais, -an)
-er verbs (-o, -es, -e, -emos, -eis, -en)
-ir verbs (-o, -es, -e, -imos, -is, -en)

The present indicative of stem changing verbs is as follows:
-ar verbs
 Example: Pensar (pienso, piensas, piensa, pensamos, pensáis, piensan)

Other stem changing verbs conjugated like pensar are:

Acertar, apretar, atravesar, cerrar, comenzar, confesar, despertar, empezar, encerrar, governar, helar, nevar, quebrar, remendar, sentar

Example: Mostrar (muestro, muestras, muestra, mostramos, mostráis, muestran)

Other stem changing verbs conjugated like mostrar are:

Acordar, acostar, almorzar, contrar, costar, encontrar, jugar (u to ue), recordar, renovar, tronar, volar
-er verbs
Example: Querer (quiero, quieres, quiere, queremos, queréis, quieren)

Other stem changing verbs conjugated like querer are:

Ascender, defender, descender, encender, entender, perder

Example: Volver (vuelvo, vuelves, vuelve, volvemos, volvéis, vuelven)

Other stem changing verbs are:

Conmover, devolver, doler, llover, mover, oler (o to hue), poder, resolver, soler
-ir verbs
Example: Consentir (consiento, consientes, consiente, consentimos, consentís, consienten)

Other stem changing verbs conjugated like consentir are:

Advertir, convertir, divertir, hervir, mentir, preferir, referir, sentir

Example: Dormir (duermo, duermes, duerme, dormimos, dormís, duermen)

Another stem changing verb conjugated like dormir is morir.

Example: Pedir (pido, pides, pide, pedimos, pedís, piden)

Other stem changing verbs conjugated like pedir are:

Despedir, gemir, impedir, medir, reir, renir, repetir, servir, sonreir, vestir

The present indicative of verbs ending in –uir is as follows:

Example: Huir (huyo, huyes, huye, huimos, huís, huyen)

The present indicative of certain verbs ending in –iar is as follows:

Example: Enviar (envio, envias, envia, enviamos, enviáis, envian)

Other verbs conjugated like enviar are confiar and espiar.

Verbs with irregular forms in the present indicative:

Decir	**Estar**	**Haber**	**Ir**
Digo	Estoy	He	Voy
Dices	Estás	Has	Vas
Dice	Está	Ha	Va
Decimos	Estamos	Hemos	Vamos
Decís	Estáis	Habéis	Váis
Dicen	Están	Han	Van

Oir	**Ser**	**Tener***	**Venir**
Oigo	Soy	Tengo	Vengo
Oyes	Eres	Tienes	Vienes
Oye	Es	Tiene	Viene
Oímos	Somos	Tenemos	Venimos
Oís	Sóis	Tenéis	Venís
Oyen	Son	Tienen	Vienen

*Also conjugated like tener are the following: contener, detener, entretener, mantener, obtener, sostener.

Verbs with irregular forms only in the first person singular of present indicative:

- Caber – yo quepo
- Dar – yo doy
- Hacer – yo hago
- Poner* – yo pongo
- Conocer** – yo conozco
- Saber – yo sé
- Salir – yo salgo
- Coger – yo cojo
- Valer – yo valgo

*Also conjugated like poner are the following:

componer, disponer, imponer, oponer, proponer

**Also conjugated like conocer are the following:

aborrecer, agradecer, aparecer, carecer, crecer, desaparecer, desconocer, establecer, estremecerse, merecer, nacer, obedecer, ofrecer, parecer, permanecer, pertenecer, reconocer

Spelling changes in the present indicative are as follows:

-verbs ending in –cer or –cir: the "c" changes to "z" before adding "o" or "a"
-verbs ending in –ger or –gir: the "g" changes to "j" before adding "o" or "a"
-verbs ending in –guir: the "gu" changes to "g" before adding "o" or "a"

The present indicative of verbs ending in –uar is as follows:

Example: Continuar (continuo, continuas, continua, continuamos, continuais, continuan)

Other verbs conjugated like continuar are actuar and graduar

Infinitives are used
- As the subject of a sentence.
- With prepositions.
- With present participles.
- With passive voice.

Uses of the preterite indicative tense:

- To express specific actions or events completed in the past
- To express a specific action or event at a specific point in time
- To state a particular action

The preterite tense of regular verbs is formed by dropping the infinitive ending and adding the following edings:

-ar verbs (-e, -aste, -o, -amos, -astéis, -aron)
-er and -ir verbs (-I, -iste, -io, -imos, -istéis, -ieron)

Verbs that end in –er and –ir and contain a vowel immediately before the ending change in the third person singular from –io to –yo.
   Exceptions: traer, atraer, and all verbs ending in –guir.

Verbs ending in –car, -gar, and –zar change in the first person singular of the preterite as follows:

"c" changes to "qu"
"g" changes to "gu"
"z" changes to "c"

Verbs that have a stem change in the present tense also have a stem change in the preterite tense.
The following verbs have an irregular stem in the preterite.

   Andar, caber, estar, haber, hacer, poder, poner, querer, saber, tener,   venir, decir, producir, traer

The endings for these verbs are –e, -iste, -o, -imos, -isteis, -ieron.
Hacer is spelled "hizo" in the third person singular.
All compounds of poner (example: proponer), tener, hacer, convenir, and traer are conjugated in the same manner as the basic verb.
All verbs ending in –ducir are conjugated like producir.

Verbs that are completely irregular in the preterite are the following:
   Dar: di, diste, dio, dimos, distéis, dieron
   Ser and Ir: fui, fuiste, fue, fuimos, fuistéis, fueron

Verbs with irregular forms in the preterite:

Tener	Andar	Poner	Querer
Tuve	Anduve	Puse	Quise
Tuviste	Anduviste	Pusiste	Quisiste
Tuvo	Anduvo	Puso	Quiso
Tuvimos	Anduvimos	Pusimos	Quisimos
Tuvisteis	Anduvisteis	Pusisteis	Quisisteis
Tuvieron	Anduvieron	Pusieron	Quisieron

Estar	Saber	Poder	Hacer
Estuve	Supe	Pude	Hice
Estuviste	Supiste	Pudiste	Hiciste
Estuvo	Supo	Pudo	Hizo
Estuvimos	Supimos	Pudimos	Hicimos
Estuvisteis	Supisteis	Pudisteis	Hicisteis
Estuvieron	Supieron	Pudieron	Hicieron

Venir	Decir	Traer	Dar
Vine	Dije	Traje	Di
Viniste	Dijiste	Trajiste	Diste
Vino	Dijo	Trajo	Dio
Vinimos	Dijimos	Trajimos	Dimos
Vinisteis	Dijisteis	Trajisteis	Distéis
Vinieron	Dijeron	Trajeron	Dieron

Ver	Ir	Ser
Vi	Fui	Fui
Viste	Fuiste	Fuiste
Vio	Fue	Fue
Vimos	Fuimos	Fuimos
Vistéis	Fuistéis	Fuistéis
Vieron	Fueron	Fueron

Uses of the imperfect tense:

- To describe what was happening, used to happen, or happened repeatedly in the past
- To describe persons or things in the past
- To tell a story, set the stage of a story
- To express a state of mind in the past
- To express past numbers, age, temperature, etc.
- To emphasize what was going on in the past when another action took place

The imperfect tense of regular verbs is formed by dropping the infinitive ending and by adding the following endings:
    Ar verbs (-aba, -abas, -aba, -abamos, -abais, -aban)
    Er and ir verbs (-ía, -ías, -ía, -íamos, -ías, -ían)

Verbs irregular in the imperfect:

    Ser (era, eras, era, éramos, erais, eran)
    Ir (iba, ibas, iba, íbamos, ibais, iban)
    Ver (veía, veías, veía, veíamos, veíais, veían)

The past participle of regular verbs is formed by dropping the infinitive ending and adding "-ado" for –ar verbs and "ido" for –er and –ir verbs.

The past participles of –er and –ir verbs with stems ending in a vowel have an accent mark.

Common verbs with irregular past participles include:

Abrir	Abierto
Cubrir	Cubierto
Escribir	Escrito
Morir	Muerto
Poner	Puesto
Romper	Roto
Ver	Visto
Volver	Vuelto
Decir	Dicho
Hacer	Hecho

Present Perfect (pretérito perfecto compuesto)

The present perfect tense is used to:

Describe an action that began in the past and continues up to the present.
Describe an action that took place in the past but in connected with the present.

This tense is formed with the present tense of haber and the past participle.

Progressive Tenses

The gerund is equivalent to the English present participle and is formed by dropping the infinitive ending and adding the following:

-ar verbs: ando   -er and –ir verbs: iendo

FOREIGN LANGUAGE: SPANISH

The gerund of –er and –ir verbs with stems ending in a vowel is formed by adding –yendo.
In the gerund, stem changing –ir verbs change the stem vowel from "e" to "i" and from "o" to "u."

Other regular gerunds are ir (yendo) and poder (pudiendo.)

The gerund is used with forms of the verbs estar, seguir, and continuar.

Future

The future tense is used to express a state of being or action that will take place some time in the future and is used to indicate*:

- Conjecture regarding the present
- Probability regarding the present
- Indirect quotations

*The future is never used after *si*, when *si* means if.

The future tense of regular verbs if formed by adding the following endings to the infinitive:

-ar, -er, and –ir verbs (-é, -ás, -á, -emos, -éis, -án)

Verbs that have accent marks in the infinitive drop that accent in the future.

Verbs like "poder" drop the "e" of the infinitive and then add the endings of the future tense. Other such verbs are "caber," "haber," "querer," and "saber."

In verbs like "poner," the "e" of the infinitive is replaced by a "d" and the endings of the future tense are added. Other such verbs are "salir," "tener," "valer," and "venir."

The verbs "decir" and "hacer" are irregular in the future tense.

Decir: diré, dirás, dirá, diremos, diréis, dirán
Hacer: haré, harás, hará, haremos, haréis, harán

Compounds of the irregular verbs are also irregular.

Conditional

The conditional tense is used to express

- An action that you would do if something else was possible.

- A conditional desire while being courteous.
- An indirect quotation.
- A conjecture regarding the past.
- A probability regarding the past.

The conditional tense of regular verbs if formed by adding the following endings to the infinitive:

-ar, -er, and –ir verbs (-ía, -ías, -ía, -íamos, -íais, -ían)

Verbs that have accent marks in the infinitive drop that accent in the conditional.

Verbs like "poder" drop the "e" of the infinitive and then add the endings of the conditional tense. Other such verbs are "caber," "haber," "querer," and "saber."

The verbs "decir" and "hacer" are irregular in the conditional tense.
Decir: diría, dirías, diría, diríamos, diríais, dirían
Hacer: haría, harías, haría, haríamos, haríais, harían

Compounds of the irregular verbs are also irregular.

* * *

The passive voice in Spanish is as follows:

True passive: Yo hice el trabajo.
or

Reflexive passive: Se hizo el trabajo.

True passive: El cogió la flor.

or

Reflexive passive: Se cogió la flor.

The use of or disuse of "se" qualifies the sentences as using a true passive voice (with "se") or a reflexive passive voice (without "se").

The impersonal tense refers to objects without a subject. They can be used with the preposition "a."
For example:

Hice trabajo.   Cogí a la flor.   Dormí bien.

Subjunctive

The subjunctive mood often clouds the facts, expresses an opinion or emotion, or indirect command. The following mnemonic device might help you to remember some of the uses:

Wish
E motion
D esire
D oubt/denial
I mpersonal expressions
N egation
G eneral commands
S peculation about the future

The present subjunctive is used if the verb in the main clause is present, future, imperative, or perfect.

Dropping the ending "-o" of the first person singular and adding the following endings form the present subjunctive of most verbs:

- -ar verbs (-é, -es, - é, emos, - é is, - én)
- -er and –ir verbs (-a, -as, -a, -amos, -áis, -an)

In verbs ending in –car, -gar, and –zar change the "c" to "qu," the "g" to "gu" and the "z" to "c."

Stem changing verbs have the same stem changes in the subjunctive as in the present indicative.

The following are irregular verbs in the subjunctive tense:

Dar	Estar	Haber	Ir	Saber	Ser
Dé	Esté	Haya	Vaya	Sepa	Sea
Des	Estes	Hayas	Vayas	Sepas	Seas
Dé	Esté	Haya	Vaya	Sepa	Sea
Demos	Estemos	Hayamos	Vayamos	Sepamos	Seamos
Déis	Estéis	Hayáis	Vayáis	Sepáis	Seáis
Dén	Estén	Hayan	Vayan	Sepan	Sea

The imperfect subjunctive is used if the verb in the main clause is imperfect, preterite, conditional, or pluperfect.

The imperfect subjunctive of all verbs is formed by dropping the –ron ending of the third person plural of the preterite tense and adding either of these endings:

- -ra, -ras, -ra, -rámos, -ráis, -ran

-se, -ses, -se, -semos, -seis, -sen

The perfect subjunctive consists of the present subjunctive of *haber* plus a past participle.
The pluperfect subjunctive consists of the imperfect subjunctive of *haber* plus a past participle.

The tense of the subjunctive depends on the form of the main verb use present subjunctive or perfect subjunctive if the verb in the main clause is in the following tenses:

- Present indicative
- Present perfect
- Future-command

Use imperfect subjunctive or pluperfect subjunctive if the verb in the main clause is in the following tenses:

- Imperfect
- Preterite
- Conditional
- Pluperfect

TEACHER CERTIFICATION EXAM

A verb is used reflexively when the subject of the verb is also its object. When a verb is reflexive, the infinitive ends in "se."

Regular cases

Llamarse
Enjabonarse
Cortarse
Acordarse
Valerse
Caerse
Callarse

Exceptional Cases

Abstengo
Arrepintió
Resigno
Condeno

Reflexive verbs are conjugated by adding the reflexive pronoun before the regular case. Excpetional cases do not need the reflexive pronoun.

For example:

Yo me llamo Jonron.

Si os acordéis de mi cara, dilo.

No nos calles, que merecemos respeto.

* * *

Nouns that end in –a, -dad, -tad, -tud, -umbre, -ie, or –ion are usually feminine.

Nouns that end in –o are usually masculine.

Nouns that end in a vowel form the plural by adding "s." Those that end in a consonant form the plural by adding –es.

Nouns ending in –z change the –z to –c before adding –es.

The verb agrees in number with the subject.

Adjectives agree in number and gender with the subject.

Definite articles - as does the English definite article "the" refer to definite persons or things already mentioned or known about. They are: "el," "la," "los," and "las."

    Singular: "el," m. "la," fem.
    Plural: "los," m. "las," fem.

Definite articles are required in Spanish and are used

- Before all nouns in a general or all-inclusive sense.
- Before titles and before adjectives preceding proper names, except in direct address.
- To translate as the English definite article "a" or "an" before proper nouns of measure or rate.
- Before names of languages except directly after "hablar" and after the prepositions "de" and "en."
- Before all geographical names modified by an adjective or adjectival phrase.

Indefinite articles, like the English definite articles "a," "an, "one,"" some," are used to mention nonspecific persons or things. They are: "un," "una," "unos," "unas."

- Singular: "un," m. "una," fem.
- Plural: "unos," .m "unas," fem.

Indefinte articles are frequently omitted in Spanish in favor of Definite articles and Subject pronouns. They are used:

- Indicate an indefinite object
- Indicate an indefinite person
- To indicate other members

They are not used:

- Before an unmodified noun after a form of "ser" (to be), especially in reference to occupation, religion, affiliation, or social status (normally, if the noun is modified, the article should be used)
- Before "otro" (other)
- Before "mil" (thousand) and "cien" (hundred)
- In exclamations using "que" (what)
- After "con" (with) and "sin" (without)
- Frequently after forms of "tener," (to have) "comprar," (to buy) "llevar," (to carry) and some other verbs when generically referring to things that people would normally have or use one at a time

Shortened Adjectives

There are several Spanish adjectives that have a shortened form when they precede certain nouns.

The most common shortened adjectives are those that drop the final -o in front of a masculine singular noun.

The following adjectives drop the final –o when used before a masculine singular noun:

- "Uno"
- "Malo"
- "Tercero"
- "Ninguno" (becomes "ningún") before masculine nouns
- "Bueno"
- "Primero"
- "Alguno" (becomes 'algún") before masculine nouns
- "Primero"
- "Tercero"

"Grande" becomes "gran" when used before a singular noun of either gender.

"Ciento" becomes "cien" when used before a noun of either gender and when multiplying numerical quantities.

"Cualquiera" becomes "cualquier" when used before a noun of either gender.

The adjective "Santo" is shortened to "San" when preceding most masculine saints' names.

Position Adjectives

The adjectives in Spanish may precede or follow the noun. As a general rule, they follow the noun, especially in the case of long adjectives, proper adjectives, adjectives used emphatically, or of any adjective which is used to call attention to some individual object, separating it from other more or less similar objects. Numeral adjectives and adjectives of quantity usually precede the noun.

Some adjectives have different meanings, depending on their position
Some of these are antiguo, cierto, grande, mismo, nuevo, probe, and simple
Limiting adjectives (numbers, possessive and demonstrative adjectives, adjectives of quantity) usually precede the noun.

Comparative Degree

When comparing the quality of two nouns, the adjective is in the comparative degree. The words más and menos do not change with gender or number.

The comparative degree may express superiority (greater than) using the construction "más" + adjective/adverb + "que" . . .

The comparative degree may express inferiority (less than) using the construction "menos" + adjective/adverb + "que" . . .

The comparative degree may express equality using the construction "tan " + adjective/adverb + "como" . . .

The words "más" and "menos" are not used with the irregular comparatives "mayor" and "peor".

Superlative Degree

The superlative degree of adjectives or adverbs is formed by putting the definite article or a possessive pronoun before the comparative. There are some constructions where simply "más," without the definite article is used, such as to form the superlative of adverbs.

Words such as "mejor" (best) and "peor" (worst) can also stand alone as superlatives.

With the irregular superlatives, the definite article is used.

Absolute Superlatives are also formed by adding the suffix –"ísimo" (-a, -os, -as) to an adjective or an adverb.

- Singular:-"isimo" m.   -"isima" fem.
- Plural: -"isimos" m.   -"isimas" fem.

Demonstrative Adjectives

Demonstrative adjectives are words which indicate a specific noun.

Singular: "ese," m. "esa," fem. "este," m. "esta," fem. "aquel," m. "aquella," fem.
Plural: "estos," m. "estas," fem. "esos," m. "esas" fem. "aquellos," m. "aquellas," fem.

- This: "este," "esta,"
- That: "ese," "esa," "aquel," "aquella"
- These: "estos," "estas,"

- Those: "ese," "esas," "aquellos," "aquellas"

The suffix -mente is added to the end of the feminine, singular form of the adjective. Generally, the feminine, singular form of the adjective is the same as the "regular" or masculine, singular form unless the adjective ends in an o, in which case the -o is changed to an -a.

Time: ahora, después, mientras, entonces, antes, pronto, tardemente.

Place: aquí, arriba, abajo, allí, acá, afuera, dentro.

Modifier: así, tranquilamente, muy,.

Afirming: sí, claro, afirmativamente.

Refusing: no, tampoco, nunca.

Quantity: mucho, casi, poco, demasiado.

Doubt: quizá, acaso, tal vez. depronto

The preposition "por" is used to express the following:

- Exchange, price, terms, units of measure, rate or multiplication
- Duration of time
- The cause, motive, or reason for an action
- The means, manner, medium or instrument by which something is done
- Indefinite or vague location
- On account of, for the sale of, on behalf of

The preposition "para" is used to express the following:

- Destination
- Purpose or use
- Comparisons or contrasts
- A definite point in future time
- After "estar" to state something is about to happen

The preposition "en" is used to express the following:

- Location
- Proportion
- Amount of time or money
- Means
- Compound prepositions
- Functional neuter expressions

The preposition "a" is used to express the following:

- To indicate motion
- To connect a verb with a following infinitive
- To indicate manner or method
- To introduce a direct object that is a definite person or treated as a person
- To introduce an indirect object
- In various expressions of time
- Preceding the pronouns (alguien, nadie, quién) when used as the direct object.

Subject Pronouns:

Singular

I: yo
You: tú, usted, vos
He: él
She: ella

Plural

We: nosotros, m. nosotras fem.
You: vosotros, m. vosotras fem. ustedes
They: ellos, m. ellas fem.

Subject pronouns are used for emphasizing or for clarifying the object.

The English pronoun "It" has no Spanish equivalent.

The reflexive pronoun is another form of an object pronoun, either direct or indirect. It indicates that the subject and the object of the verb are the same person or thing.

Reflexive pronouns (me, te, se, nos, os, se) generally precede the verb in simple and compound tenses or they may be tacked onto the end of verbs which are in the infinitive, gerund, or command forms.

The final –d in a vosotros verb command form, replacing –r at the end of the infinitive, is dropped if the reflexive pronoun is added to the end.

Object pronouns (le, lo, la, los, les, las) are attached to affirmative commands.

With affirmative commands introduced by que, the object pronoun always precedes the verb.

Certain verbs are often used with indirect object pronouns. They are gustar, agradar, bastar, doler, faltar, hacer, faltar, parecer, placer, quedar, sobrar, and tocar.

When a verb has two object pronouns, the indirect object pronoun precedes the direct object pronoun.

FOREIGN LANGUAGE: SPANISH

-Le and –les change to "se" before lo, la, los, and las are added.

The preposition "a" is used before the direct object of a verb if the direct object is
- A definite person or persons
- A domestic animal
- A geographic name
- A pronoun referring to a person

Demonstrative Pronouns

This: "éste," "ésta," "esto"
That: "ése," "ésa," "eso," "aquel," "áquella" "aquéllo"
These: "éstos," "éstas,"
Those: "ése," "ésas," "aquéllos," "aquéllas"

For Example:

- Si éste fue, hubieramos Ganado.

- No quiero eso.

- Èsa es mi favorite.

Relative Pronouns

Relative Pronouns are used to introduce the clause of a sentence that describes the noun throughtout the rest of the sentence.

Que	quien	quienes	donde	cuyo –ya, cuyos –yas	el que, la que	lo que
who-tha	who	whom	where	whose	which	who

los que las que	el cual la cual	lo cual	los cuales las cuales
whom	who	which	whom.

For Example:

- Si es que no me das tu bendición; no hay suerte.

- Con quienes viajé viniste bien acompañada.

- Èl, que sabe todo, nos ayudara.

- Quienes vivan, quienes respiren, son mis hermanos.

- Cuyos problemas siguieron sin nunca parar, estarás bien.

Possessive Pronouns

Mi, mis	su, sus	tu, tus	nuestro-as	vuestros -as
My	*your*	*his*	*ours*	*yours*

mío –a, míos -as	suyo –yas,	tuyo- yas
Mine	*yours*	*yours*

For Example:

- Quédese con sus propias necesidades, las mías estan tranquilas.

- Tú y tus animales se pueden ir a la selva para vivir pacificamente.

- El mundo es tuyo y de mis hijos será siempre más.

- Con quien se volteé a mirar la bestia en los ojos, suyo será el premio final.

- Su libro esta muy bueno.

- Mirenme y veran nuestros antepasados en su extension total.

- Me caigo y la culpa fue tuya.

Al

The contraction of the prepositions "a" and "el."

Del

The contraction of the prepositions "el" and "de."

For Example:

Nos vamos al campo.

Al correr se respira.

Al mundo no se llora.

Antes del primer de enero ire a comer sushi.

Compre carne del carnicero.

TEACHER CERTIFICATION EXAM

Conjunctions

Y, e, u	and
O	or
Ni	nor
Pero	but

For Example:

Esta bien, pero solo por una razón u la otra.

Jaime y Jairo fueron caminando a la tienda.

Si no lo quieres ni lo pienses hacer.

Fueron sólo los rojos e anaranjados que desaparecieron ayer.

E incluso, mi madre me dijo que estuve bien en terminar mi

Quieres que vaya o no.

* * *

When a noun's quantity is only one, use "un –a" for either masculine or feminine forms.

"Cien" is one hundred. When combined with other numbers of lesser quanties it becomes "ciento" or plural, "cientos" (e.g., ciento dos, ocho cientos, cuatro cientos cincuenta y ocho). It does not use "y" to connect with other quantities. "Mil" is one thousand and stays so no matter how it is combined.

Numbers greater than 999 are written with a period for every greater set of numbers, not a comma. "Millón" is one million. For written quantities that do not include values in any places lesser than the millions value place a "de" is attached to the noun (e.g., cuatro millones de gatos, not cuatro millones tres gatos). There are no written designations for quantities larger than millions. A billion would be written: "mil millones." A trillion would be written" "mil millones de millones."

The days of the week, months, and seasons are not capitalized in Spanish. Dates are written day, month, year. When writing out the first day of the month use "el primer día" or "el primero," otherwise, use cardinal numbers (e.g., domingo, quince de marzo; martes, catorce de enero…)

Went:

Fue, Fueron, Fui, Fuimos, Fuiste, Fuistéis

For Example:

Te quiero.
¿Me quieres?

Love:

Amo, Amar, Quiero, Quieres

I love you.
Do you love me?

Going:

Iba, ibas, ibamos, ibais, iban

Tenga
Also used as
Ten

For Example:

Tenga mis hijos. [Ten]

Quiero que lo tenga.

Venga
Also used as
Ven

For Example:

Venga a mi casa. [Ven}

No me venga con esas cosas.

Negative Constructions

The word "no" is placed before a verb to make a negative meaning. "No" is repeated to affirm the negative construction to a yes or no question.

For Example:

-¿Quieres correr?
-No, no me gusta correr.

TEACHER CERTIFICATION EXAM

Interrogative Constructions

Qué

Inquires actions and for replies.

Cúal, Cuáles

Inquires statements.

Quién, Quiénes

Inquires for person.

Cuánto, Cuánta, Cuántos, Cuántas,

Inquires quantity.

Cómo

Inquires occurrence.

* * *

As in English, commands are used when telling someone what to do.

How to form commands:

- The polite commands (singular and plural) have the same form as the present subjunctive.
- The singular of the familiar command is the same as the third person singular of the present indicative.
- Object pronouns are added to all affirmative commands
- All negative commands have the same form as the corresponding person in the present subjunctive.
- In negative commands, the object pronouns precede the verb.
- Indirect commands are always expressed by the present subjunctive and are usually introduced by "que."

The only irregular commands occur in the affirmative singular (tú) and are as follows:

- Decir – di
- Hacer – haz
- Ir – ve
- Poner – pon

FOREIGN LANGUAGE: SPANISH

- Salir – sal
- Ser – sé
- Tener – ten
- Valer – val
- Venir – ven

*   *   *

Tuve chance tanto de vivir de que morir.

Comparative Equality.

Ella quiso tanto sus chances de comer lasaña que entonó un alarido.

Comparative Equality.

No me digas tanto.

Comparative Equality.

Vale menos.

Comparativen Inequality.

La molécula es pequeñísima.

Absolute Superlative.

El Elefante es grandísimo.

Absolute Superlative.

El restaurante durará tanto que estaré cocinando en la próxima vida.

Comparative Equality.

Mi casa es tan buena.

Comparative Inequality.

Si entiendes que es mejor.

Comparative Inequality.

No quize ser el peor de todos tus amigos.

Comparative Inequality.

Tanta fue que no la puedes echar de menos.

Comparative Equality.

Por lo menos estuve cerca a la meta.

Comparative Inequality.

0010 Understand processes involved in second- and heritage-language acquisition.

Stephen Krashen's Language Acquisition Theory states acquisition and learning are two separate processes. Learning is knowing about a language – formal knowledge; acquisition is the unconscious mind related activity that occurs when the language is used in conversation. He embodies the following hypotheses in his theory:

- **A.** Natural Order: Natural progression/order of language development exhibited by infants/young children and/or second language learners (child or adult).

    Level I: Pre-Production Stage (Silent Period): Minimal comprehension, no verbal production.

    Level II: Early Production Stage. Limited Comprehension; One/two-word response.

    Level III: Speech Emergence Stage. Increased comprehension; Simple sentences; Some errors in speech.

    Level IV: Intermediate Fluency Stage. Very good comprehension; More complex sentences; Complex errors in speech.

- **B.** Monitor: Learning (as opposed to acquisition) serves to develop a monitor- an error detecting mechanism that scans utterances for accuracy in order to make corrections. As a corollary to the monitor hypothesis, language acquisition instruction should avoid emphasis on error correction and grammar. Such an emphasis might inhibit language acquisition, particularly at the early stages of language development.

- **C.** Input: Input needs to be comprehensible. Input + 1/Zone of Proximal Development- Input/instruction that is just above the students' abilities. Instruction that is embedded in a meaningful context, modified (paraphrasing, repetition), collaborative/ interactive and multimodal.

- **D.** Affective Filter: Optimal input occurs when the "affective filter" is low The affective filter is a screen of emotion that can block language acquisition or learning if it keeps the users from being too self-conscious or too embarrassed to take risks during communicative exchanges.

In addition, the Cultural Adaption / Cultural Shock cycle for students, upon introducing themselves to a new language and its culture is to experience the following:

1. Honeymoon: The sojourner is intrigued by the differences she or he perceives and is excited about everything.

2. Disintegration: The differences between the cultures lead to confusion, isolation and loneliness. New cultural cues are misread and withdrawal and depression can occur.

3. Re-integration: The new cues are re-integrated but even though the individual has an increased ability to function in the new culture, he rejects it and experiences anger and resentment and acts hostile and rebellious.

4. Autonomy: The person is able to see the differences between the two cultures in a more objective way, is able to deal with them and therefore feels more self-assured, relaxed and confident.

5. Independence: The social psychological and cultural differences are accepted and enjoyed (ibid.). And the person is able to function in both the old and the new culture; he has achieved bi-culturality.

SUBAREA IV—CULTURAL KNOWLEDGE

0011 Demonstrate familiarity with manners, customs, and ranges of cultural expression in various Spanish-speaking communities.

Most Spanish dialects have two second person singular pronouns, one for informal use and one for more formal treatment. In most dialects the informal pronoun is "tú," which comes directly from the Latin, and the formal pronoun is "usted," which is usually considered to originate from "vuestra merced," (Your grace) -though others have traced it to the - Arabic "Ustad, professor/sir."

In a number of regions "tú" is replaced by another pronoun "vos" and the verb conjugation changes accordingly "Vos" comes from Latin "vos," which was simply the second person plural informal pronoun.

In Spain "tú" is informal -to friends and "usted" is formal -to elders. In parts of Spain fifty years ago a child would not use "tú" but "usted," to address a parent. Chileans employ "usted" to address children to parents and also parents to children. In Cuba "tú" is used even in very formal circumstances and "usted" remains seldom used. In most of inland Colombia "usted" is the pronoun of choice for all situations even when speaking between friends or family, but in the country's capital the use of "tú" is more accepted in informal situations, especially between young interlocutors of the opposite sex and among young women. In the Caribbean coast "tú" is used for practically all informal situations and many formal situations, "usted" being reserved for the most formal environments.

Tuteo:

Is using the second person singular pronoun "tú" informally, especially in contexts where "usted" is to be grammatically expected. The notion's corresponding verb is "tutear": a transitive verb. *Tuteo* is used even in those dialects where the informal pronoun is "vos." It is prevalent in Chile, Cuba, and Colombia. It is used particularly to address family or friends and adds an intimate tone to personal reference.

Joan Corominas explains that "vos" was the peasant form in classical Castilian and being that most Spanish immigrants to the New World belonged to this class, "vos" became the unmarked, present form.

Voseo:

Is the use of the second person singular pronoun "vos" in several dialects of Spanish, instead of "tú," which is often considered standard. "

Vos" is used extensively as the primary spoken form of the second-person singular in various countries around Latin America, including Argentina, Costa Rica, Ecuador, El Salvador, Guatemala, Honduras, the Zulia State, Venezuela, various regions of Colombia. Nicaragua, Paraguay and Uruguay, but only in Argentina, Uruguay, and increasingly in Paraguay, is it also the standard written form. This phenomenon is also gradually taking place in Central America, where the most prestigious media outlets are beginning to use the pronoun "vos" instead of "tú."

Ceceo:

Is a phenomenon in the Spanish language whereby "th" is enounced instead of "s." It is a standard feature of Castilian Spanish.

- Buenos días: Good morning
- Por Favor: Please
- Señor, Señora, Señorita: Mr., Mrs., Miss
- Permítame presentarle a Vd.: Allow me to introduce you to
- Encantado: (…)Delighted
- Gracias: Thank You
- De nada: You are welcome
- No hay de que: Do not mention it
- Hasta la vista: So long
- El gusto es mío: The pleasure is mine
- Adíos: Good bye
- Hasta mañana: See you tomorrow
- ¿Cómo está?: How are you?
- Está bien: It's all right
- En la estación de tren: At the railway station
- Pásame cinco dolares: Pass five dollars to me
- Limpia tu cuarto: Clean your room
- Salgase del vehículo: Exit the vehicle
- Váyase a casa: Go home
- Entra a mi casa: Come into my house
- Usa el computador: Use the computer
- Llévame a un restaurante: Take me to a restaurant
- Cómprate un vestido: Buy yourself a dress
- Cocina el desayuno: Cook breakfast
- Venga a mi casa: Come to my house
- ¿Puedo entrar?: Can I come in?
- Permiso: Excuse me

MONEY FROM SPANISH SPEAKING COUNTRIES

Country	Currency
Spain	Euro
Colombia	Colombian Peso
Venezuela	Bolivariano
Ecuador	U.S. Dollar
Peru	"Nuevo" Sole
Bolivia	Boliviano
Chile	Chilean Peso
Uruguay	Uruguayan Peso
Paraguay	Guaraní
Argentina	Argentine Peso
Panamá	U.S. Dollar
Costa Rica	Costa Rican Colón
Guatemala	Quetzale
El Salvador	El Salvadorian Colón
Honduras	Lempira
Nicaragua	Cordoba
Mexico	Mexican Peso
Cuba	Cuban Peso
Dominican Republic	Dominican Republic Peso
Puerto Rico	U.S. Dollar

0012 Demonstrate familiarity with the arts (e.g., music, dance, folk, art, visual art, drama, architecture) and literature of various Spanish-speaking communities.

Alfonso X is the most prominent figure in Spanish literature of the Middle Ages. He brought together the most learned men of those times to translate and write texts on various subjects such as history and astronomy.

In the fourteenth century, cowboy novels began to appear. These satires described the supernatural adventures of its heroes. In the fifteenth century, poetry became popular.

Jorge Manrique is a famous poet who wrote poetry to honor his father. Henry Wadsworth Longfellow has translated his work into English.

Antonio de Nebrija is famous for having written the first Spanish grammar book.

The Golden Age is the most glorious era of Spanish literature.

Garcilaso de la Vega was a soldier and poet who truly represented the Renaissance. He introduced Spain to various new forms of poetry such as the sonnet.

The sixteenth century has several satirical novels worth mentioning.

Miguel de Cervantes Saavedra is most famous for having written "Don Quixote," which is one of the world's most read books –printed in several languages. This is a satirical novel whose underlying message was the conflict between idealism and materialism. Cervantes was a soldier who lost the use of his left arm in a war. Pirates held him prisoner for five years. He was unlucky in both marriage and business, having spent years in prison because of a bad business deal. Lope de Vega wrote all types of works but his most famous were dramas. It is said that he is the father of the modern comedy as well as the creator of the National Theatre of Spain.

This era also saw various other writers such as: Francisco de Quevedo, a satirical writer; Juan Ruiz de Alarcón, a Mexican whose plays put down vices, honor and virtue; Tirso de Molina, who was a Spaniard famous for having created Don Juan; Pedro Calderon de la Barca, whose plays deal primarily with honor.

In 1713, the Academy of the Spanish Language was created. Its primary purpose was to maintain the purity of the Spanish language. This era also saw the beginnings of romanticism.

José de Espronceda was a romantic poet who has been compared to Lord Byron. Mariano José de Larra was a very famous critical essayist who wrote under various pen names. José Zorrilla is most famous for having written a drama based on Don Juan from a romantic perspective. Gustavo Adolfo Becquet wrote many lyrical poems.

Romanticism was followed by idealism. Fernán Caballero is the creator of "costumbrista" novels. The purpose of these types of books was to criticize or poke fun at the customs of certain regions.

Juan Valera presented a poetic vision of his home, the region of Andalucía. Benito Pérez Galdós is considered the most important Spanish novelists of the nineteenth century. He was a violent critic of religious intolerance and of social injustice.

Emilio Pardo Bazán introduced naturalism and established contact between European and Spanish literature.

He mainly wrote about his home, the region of Galicia. Armando Palacio Valdés was a popular novelist who wrote about the region of Andalucía and about the fisherman of Asturias.

Vicente Blasco Ibañez was popular not only in Spain but all over the world. He was a great defender of republican ideas and of individual freedom. He was imprisoned on several occasions because of his political ideas.

Ruben Darío was a Nicaraguan poet who was known as the "Prince of Spanish Literature" or the "Father of Modernism" by other great Spanish writers. His poems are a mix of traditionalism, romanticism and the poetic substance which is created from fusing such themes.

Because of the War of 1898, Spain lost what was left of its colonial empire. In the wake of this disaster, a group of young, Spanish intellectuals got together to examine the cultural and spiritual state of their country. They called themselves, the Generation of '98.

Francisco Giner de los Ríos was a philosopher, professor, and great educator of intellectuals. He founded "La Escuela Libre de Enseñanza," which is a center of liberal ideas.

Miguel de Unamuno was a philosopher, a critic, a poet, and a novelist. One of his favorite topics was the gap that exists between faith and reason, and between lack of faith and the desire for immortality.

Ramón del Valle-Inclán was famous for the richness of his language. His prose can practically be called poetry. In the world of theatre, Jacinto Benavente is a well-known name. This dramatist won the Nobel Prize for Literature, in 1922.

Ramón Menéndez Pidal was a very important Spanish scholar in the twentieth century. He wrote several studies on medieval language and literature in Spain.

Pío Baroja was the principal novelist of the "Generación del '98." His novels contain a lot of action. José Martínez Ruiz wrote essays and novels. His works compare the old Spain to the modern one in a simple and natural language.

Antonio Machado was on of the most loved and respected poets of this century. His poems are short but deal with fundamental themes. He introduced Ruben Darío's modernism in Spanish poetry.

Gregorio Martínez Sierra was most famous for having created notable female characters in his works. José Ortega y Gasset was a philosopher and essayist who sought to depict Spain's spiritual values and traditions.

The Civil War in Spain had as profound an effect on literature as on daily life. Many writers were against the dictatorship of Franco and left the country to continue their writing in other countries. Some were incarcerated and condemned to die.

Juan Ramón Jimenez is known as the creator of "pure poetry". He relocated to Puerto Rico where he resided when he was awarded the Nobel Prize for Literature, in 1956. Besides his many poems, he also wrote books in prose.

Federico García Lorca was a poet and dramatist who focused on folkloric themes and traditions. His theatrical work deals with human passion.

Jorge Guillén was known for writing "pure" poetry, which is poetry created from concepts and abstractions. He taught in many universities worldwide including Harvard and Wellesley College.

Vicente Aleixandre was an essayist and poet who received the Nobel Prize for Literature, in 1977. His poetry is romantic and surrealistic at the same time, with love as its central theme. Alejandro Casona was a dramatist who left Spain and settled in Argentina.

After the Civil War a group of writers emerged who had experienced the atrocities of the war firsthand. Their writing reflected the influence of the war in their preoccupation with social problems and the economy.

Julian Marías is a contemporary philosopher and essayist. He has taught at the University of Madrid, Harvard, Yale, and the University of California in Los Angeles.

Camilo José Cela is the most famous contemporary Spanish novelist. His writing possesses a mocking tone. Antonio Buero Vallejo wrote plays that modernized and gave dignity to Spanish theatre.

Miguel Delibes is a novelist who using simple language gives the reader a picture of the reality of Spanish society and of the humble man. Carmen Laforet won the Nobel Prize for Literature with a very controversial publication that dealt with the lack of spirituality in Spain after the war.

José Hierro is one of the most notable poets of the postwar era. His humanitarian poetry is deep without using imagery. Alfonso Sastre is a dramatist who writes about society with the goal of sending a message to the public. Juan Goytisolo is another important contemporary novelist. He presents the problems and uncertainties of the times in his writings. Antonio Gala is a poet and dramatist that presents modern themes using historical characters.

Gabriel García Márquez is the foremost proponent of the literary style dubbed "Magic Realism": the casual meshing of supernatural and everyday events.

He is a pioneer of the Latin-American "Boom" and was given the Nobel Prize for Literature in 1982, for the novel "Cien Años de Soledad" (One Hundred Years of Solitude). He is Colombia's most accomplished author and writes extensively in novels, short stories, and articles on the history and the mosaic picture of its daily life.

Jorge Luis Borges is Argentina's most prolific writer. His intellectually based themes are written in the form of short stories that compound philosophy and the entire universe of its ideas.

Gabriela Mistral is a Chilean educator, poet, and diplomat whose wonderfull works of poetry are conformed by contemplations of death, faith, and motherhood. She was Latin-America's first Nobel Prize winner, receiving it in 1945 for literature.

Octavio Paz was a Mexican poet and writer, whose focus in his writings tended to the union of civil liberty and nature and its corresponding love. He is Mexico's most prestigious poet of the twentieth century. He won the Nobel Prize for Literature, in 1990.

Pablo Neruda was a Chilean Poet who wrote poetry that's main theme is the historical power of Latin America and its reflection within its vitality and living soul. He was the Nobel Prize Laureate, in 1971.

Sor Juana Inés de la Cruz was a nun from Mexico: famous for being one of the most prodigious scholars of all times. She wrote poetry and prose that affirmed women's strength and their individual rights.

Spain is rich in folkloric music. Flamenco is perhaps its most famous contribution. It comes from the region of Andalucía and is a mixture of Arab, gypsy, and Jewish music of the fourteenth century. It consists of a song accompanied by guitar music and an improvised dance.

The traditional instrument of Spain is the guitar, both in traditional and modern music. For accompaniment, the tambourine and castanets are often used.

Spain has given the world music known as the zarzuela. It is a combination of music, song, spoken dialogue, choruses and dance. The most famous composers of this type of music are Francisco Asenjo Barbieri and Tomás Breton.
The four most famous Spanish composers are Isaac Albeniz, Enrique Granados and Manuel de Falla. Albeniz composed operas and piano music. Granados also composed piano music. De Falla was the most famous Spanish composer of the twentieth century. He focused on orchestra music and also wrote a few ballets. The fourth was the blind composer, Joaquín Rodrigo and his famous Concierto de Aranjuéz.

Spain has also given the world some famous instrumentalists. Among these, we find Pablo Casals, José Iturbi, Andrés Segovia and Alicia de Larrocha. Casals was one of the most famous violoncellists in the world. He left Spain in 193, because he was against the dictatorship of Franco. He settled in Puerto Rico and began an international music festival that is still held in his honor yearly. Iturbi was a pianist and director of a symphonic orchestra. He also acted in several Hollywood movies. Segovia was one of the most famous guitarists the world has ever known. De Larrocha is a famous contemporary pianist known for her interpretation of great Spanish composers as well as other famous composers.

Victoria de los Ángeles, Alfredo Krauss, Plácido Domingo, and José Carreras are famous Spanish operatic singers. Sarita Montiel, Julio Iglesias, Raphael, Camilo Sexto, Rocío Jurado and countless others are more contemporary Spanish singers.

El Prado is the most famous museum in Spain. It is located in Madrid.

There are many famous Spanish painters. Domenico Theotocopoulos, known as El Greco, was born in Crete. He studied in Italy and later moved to Spain. He lived in Toledo until his death. His work is characterized by religious undertones and by the way he lengthens his figures. José de Ribera was born in Spain but spent most of his life in Italy. His work is characterized by its realism and also his use of light and dark. Francisco de Zurbarán painted religious works in a sober and religious way. Diego Velázquez painted portraits for Felipe IV and the royal family. He also painted portraits of other Spanish nobles. Bartolomé Ésteban Murillo was a religious painter who painted things like the Immaculate Conception. Francisco de Goya y Lucientes was the most famous painter of his time. He was the painter of Carlos III and IV. Ignacio Zuluaga drew realistic pictures of people of the times like toreadors and gypsies. José María Sert is famous for his murals that depict Don Quixote. Pablo Picasso was born and educated in the Spanish province of Málaga, but spent most of his life in other parts of Spain. He began the style know as cubism, a style that rejects traditional perspective. Joan Miró is one of the most famous representatives of abstract art combined with surrealism. His works are testament to his vivid imagination. Salvador Dalí was also a surrealist. His works represent the creativity of his subconscious mind with detail and vision.

Latin-American Art

When the conquistadors arrived in the early fifteenth century, they found a very advanced art form left behind by the Indians. They had made pyramids, palaces and temples. They had made statues of their gods out of gold and silver and had made jewelry out of precious stones. They had also made elaborate pottery.

The Spaniards brought a religious form of art to the New World, which served to convert the Indians to Catholicism.

One of the most famous Mexican painters is Diego Rivera. He began his early career influenced by cubism and post-impressionism. In his twenties, he decided to dedicate himself to painting murals that represented political and social themes. His murals can be seen today decorating many public buildings in Mexico.

José Clemente Orozco was also a Mexican muralist who depicted the Mexican Revolution in his paintings. He also painted the frescos of the Palace of the Arts in Mexico City and can also be found in the United States in Dartmouth College.

David Alfaro Siqueiros was a Mexican painter famous for his expression of idealism. He was arrested several times for his political expressions.

Rufino Tamayo was a famous Mexican painter who depicted the happiness and tragedy of his country's history. He won many international art prizes and his paintings adorn famous public buildings like the National Palace of Beautiful Art and the Museum of Anthropology, both in Mexico City and the UNESCO building in Paris.

Miguel Covarrubias, also Mexican, was famous both in his country and in the United States as a painter of caricatures. His drawings have been printed in several magazines.
Cesáreo Bernaldo de Quirós was an Argentinean impressionist whose paintings represented the life of a "gaucho." His paintings depict the history of the "Pampas."

Wilfredo Lam was a Cuban surrealist painter. His paintings contained Afro-Cuban elements. Some of his works are on display in the Museum of Modern Art in New York City.

Some other artists: Emilio Pettoruti, an Argentinean cubist painter; Roberto Matta, a Chilean surrealist; Oswaldo Guayasamin, an Ecuatorian cubist; Alejandro Obregón, a Colombian abstract painter; Rómulo Macció, a vanguard Argentinean painter; Fernando Botero, a Colombian figurative painter; Gerardo Chávez, a Peruvian surrealist.

Most Hispanic music is a conjunction of rhythyms brought by African slaves to the Caribbean or native rhythyms and melodies preexisting in various indigenous cultures transplanted to the Western instruments brought by the Spanish. Salsa, Merengue, Calypso, Mambo, Cumbia and Vallenato are mixed African and western musical genres that originate in Puerto Rico, Cuba, the Dominican Republic, Honduras, Guatemala, El Salvador, Panamá and the coasts of Venezuela and Colombia. Inland in Mexico, Mariachi and Ranchera music are original and popular musical genres.

Within Peru, Colombia, Ecuador, Bolivia, Uruguay, Paraguay, Chile and Argentina Andean music "Música Andina," a genre representing native indigenous musical rhythyms and melodies, is frequently played and listened to. In Argentina, the music of choice and the genre most listened to is tango: a song and dance form both classical and folkloric; it is a profound dance technique for couples to participate in. It is developed from the expression of Argentinian and Uruguayan folklore.

0013 Demonstrate familiarity with the history, geography, demographics, and economics of various areas where Spanish is spoken.

Spain

Spain is a product of all the different civilizations that have invaded it and brought their own language and culture within. The Iberians of Mediterranean origin were the first, followed by the Celts who were of central European origin. Next the Phoenicians from the north of Africa established colonies in the south of the peninsula. They were an advanced culture who introduced writing, metal works and the idea of using money into Spain. In the seventh century B.C. the Greeks established some colonies on the Oriental coast and introduced the cultivation of grapes and olives. The Carthaginians entered the peninsula in the sixth century B.C. They conquered the Phoenicians and acquired most of the peninsula. The Roman legions conquered the Carthaginians in 202 B.C. in what we know as the Punic Wars. The Romans stayed in Spain for six centuries during in which time they greatly shaped Spanish culture. They laid the foundation for the language, the law system, and the economic and social structures that remained. They built large aqueducts, bridges and many other public works. They founded cities and built schools, theatres and outdoor arenas. They also made Christianity and the Church as the more prominent way of life.

The Muslims began invading southern Spain in 711. They defeated the Visigoths, who then had control of the south. In 718, the Visigoths defeated the Muslims and regained control. Thus began a constant war between the Moors and the Christians that continued until 1492. Thanks to Arab influence, Spain became the most advanced and cultured country in Europe. The Moors brought their architecture, their art and their irrigation system. Córdoba (the Moorish capital) became a center for scholars from around the world to study math, science and medicine. In 1094, the Christians defeated the Moors in Valencia and Rodrigo Díaz de Vivar, known as "el Cid Campeador" ruled there until 1099 when he died after being defeated by the Muslims in Cuenca.

In 1469, Isabel, princess of Castilla married Ferdinand, prince of Aragon. She later became Queen of Castilla and he the King of Aragon. They became known as "los Reyes Católicos" (The Catholic Kings). Together they defeated Boabdil, the last Moorish King in Granada. They reorganized the inquisition and expelled the Jews from Spain.

Spain then became the first nation of Europe under the reign of "Los Reyes Católicos." To expand its territory Queen Isabel first agreed to help Christopher Columbus with his endeavor to the New World; others also helped expand the Spanish empire. Among these was Gonzalo Fernandez de Córdoba, known as "el Gran Capitán." He conquered part of Italy in the name of Spain. During the reign of Carlos V (1517 – 1556), grandson of Ferdinand and Isabel, the Spanish nation acquired possessions in Germany, Austria, Italy, America, and North Africa. In 1556, Carlos V retired to a monastery and turned the empire over to his son, Felipe II, who ruled until 1598. Felipe's reign and its subsequent efforts to propagate Christianity saw the end of the Ottoman Empire in the Mediterranean and the incorporation of Portugal into the Kingdom of Spain after the death of King Sebastian, to whom Carlos V was closely related, in 1578. The destruction of its "la Armada Invincible" (The Invincible Armada), in 1588 by England, was a foreboding to the end of Spain's expansion into external territories.

Felipe II died in 1598 and his successors, Felipe III and IV, proved to be less than capable than ruling an empire of such great size. Spain suffered many losses of land. Spain was in economic ruin due to its countless wars, the immigration of its people to the New World and the expulsion of the Jews and the Moors.

The first Spanish republic which was established in 1873, lasted only 11 months. During this time it passed through four presidencies. In 1898, by way of the Treaty of Paris Spain lost possession of Cuba, Puerto Rico, the Philippines and Guam.

The second republic was declared in 1931, after Primo de Rivera - a previous dictator, was overthrown and lasted only five years because of various political battles. During the second republic Spain drafted a new constitution. The socialist republic that ensued then forced the king to flee and the right wings' groups assumed the power of the general government starting with a victory in parliament, in 1933. In 1936, "The Republican Popular Front" – the right wing coalition with elements from the left, won the elections; setting off a civil war between themselves and the insurgent Nationalist element of their government, then led by General Francisco Franco; the latter which was assisted by both Italy and Germany in effecting his military coup. He defeated the republic's forces and established a dictatorship, in 1939 that lasted until his death, in 1975. Soon after, King Juan Carlos became the new head of state. He began to dismantle the totalitarian apparatus and ushered in the democratic element of current Spanish government.

Indian Civilizations

Mayan – the most advanced of the Indian civilizations. They flourished from the third century to the sixteenth. The Mayans occupied what is now the Yucatán Peninsula, Belize, Guatemala and parts of Honduras and El Salvador. They were a very advanced culture in science, astronomy and mathematics. They had made a calendar that managed to calculate with incredible accuracy, the duration of a solar year. They also had invented the numeral zero. They were also the only Indian civilization to create a system of writing to record influential events.

Aztec – moved to the central Mexican valley in the twelfth century, remaining there until the sixteenth. They were an ambitious and religious people who had managed to conquer every tribe in the central Mexican valley and were still increasing their territory when the Spanish invaded them. They built large city-states and were the first civilization to practice mandatory education for all, regardless of gender or social status. All males were put in the army, from seventeen to twenty-two and even peasants could rise to the rank of officer, if they worked hard enough. Their enormous capital Tenochtitlán, with a population of 500,000, had causeways and canals surrounding it.

Inca – At the height of the Incan empire it was the largest empire on earth and remains the largest state to have ever existed in the Western Hemisphere. Cuzco, its capital "The Navel of the World," was the richest city in the New World. Their empire was located in the Andes and extended from Ecuador to central Chile, including parts of Bolivia and Argentina. The center of their nation was in Peru. They had an extensive political and social system. The Incans were also known for their royal family, well-organized army, and system of roads. They spoke Quechua, a language that is still spoken in parts of Peru, Bolivia, Ecuador, and northern Chile.

Lesser Civilizations – In the Caribbean, at the time of Columbus's discovery of the Antilles, there were many Indian tribes living on those Islands that were similiarly featured and related: the Arawaks, Taíno, and "Caribes" or Carib; numbering two to three million they were reduced to mere thousands by the conquistadors. In the mountains of Colombia, the "Chibchas" were the dominant civilization. A calm and religious people, famed for their expertise in their workings with gold and the rituals: such as "el Dorado" (The Golden One), that revolved around it. Their works can be seen in the "el Museo de Oro" (The Gold Museum), in Bogotá. The "Guaraniés," in Paraguay spoke Guaraní, which is still spoken in certain parts of Paraguay. The "Araucanos" or "Mapuches" in Chile and Argentina, between the Bío Bío River and the Toltén River, were a warrior-tribe that resisted both the Incan Empires' and the conquistador's advances.

In 1503, the "Casa de Contratación" (House of Trade), was organized in Seville, Spain as the centre for tax recollection and commercial regulation over the crown's property: such being the many colonies. In 1524, the Crown of Castille incorporated the new domains into the existing administrating organ of the "Consejo de Castilla" (Council of Castille), with Juan Rodríguez Fonseca as its head, resulting in the creation of the "Consejo de Indias" (Council of the Indies) and the "Real y Supremo Consejo de Indias" (Royal and Supreme Council of the Indies); priests and lawyers administered all colonies in America and the Phillipines. Combining legislative, executive, and judicial functions under one organ of command it reported to the king weekly decisions over issues that would have been handled previously by the "Casa de contratación" (House of Trade). In 1680, the council's decisions were formally codified. In 1714, Borbon reforms enacted the creation of new posts: the "Ministro de Indias" (Minister of the Indies) and the "Secretario de Guerra, Marina e Indias," (Secretary of War, Navy and Indies), to assume the authority of the old council. The colonies were divided into four administrative territories. They were as follows: 1) New Spain, which included Mexico, Central America, part of the United States and the Antilles, 2) Peru and Chile, 3) New Granada, which included Ecuador, Colombia, Panama and Venezuela and 4) "Río de la Plata," which included Argentina, Bolivia, Paraguay, Uruguay and part of Brazil. A viceroy appointed by the king of Spain governed each.

The Spanish crown had two main goals: to civilize the Indians and convert them to Catholicism and to exploit the riches of the colonies for the sole benefit of Spain.

Spanish society was divided into four classes:

1) The Spaniards, who governed and enjoyed all privileges
2) The "criollos" (of Spanish origin but born in the colonies), who were well-off financially but could not govern
3) The mestizos (the mixture of a Spaniard and a Indian), mulattos (the mixture of a Spaniard and a Black Slave), and zambo (the mixture of a Indian and a Black slave); who had no social category nor political rights
4) The Native Indians and Black slaves.

Independence

The inhabitants of the colonies grew tired of social and political injustice and of the economic restrictions placed on them by Spain. They were encouraged to seek their independence by three occurrences: the independence of the United States, the French Revolution, and the invasion of Spain by Napoleon's forces. There were four major revolutionary movements. They are:

Mexico – In 1808 Napoleon installed his brother Joseph into the throne as the King of Spain. In the colony that consisted of modern day Mexico, conservative criollos found their beliefs and values at odds with the liberal agenda of the newly installed French government and the local governors who adhered to its rule. Resistance sprang up: allegiance to the former King of Spain, Fernando VII, served as a spark for the "Grito de Dolores" (Cry of Dolores), beginning the Mexican revolution. Initiated on September 16, 1810, by Miguel Hidalgo, a priest at his own parish in the town of Dolores under the banner of the Virgin of Guadalupe, it attracted both followers and victory. The revolution led by himself, his wife and his partner Ignacio Allende, marched towards Mexico City. Reaching the edge of the city, threatening to invade it, Hidalgo turned back and they were both eventually executed, in 1811. José María Morelos, a priest as well, became the new leader of the revolutionary movement. He occupied Oaxaca in November 24, 1812. He invoked the first Mexican national congress in Chilpancingo, Guerrero, in 1813: it adopted a manifesto that elected him Generalissimo and granted him executive powers. He was in order to possess his hometown of Valladolid (now called Morelia in his honor), but was defeated and hindered into retreat; leading to his execution, in 1815, after being found by a royalist patrol led by a former follower. After losing its principal leader, Vincente Guerrero resurged as the new head of the revolutionary movement and was named protector of the independent Mexican congress. He moved the congress to Tehuacán and in 1818, he defeated General Armiso. This led to the announcement, in 1819, between himself and viceroy Apocada, to hold talks over an armistice between the government and the revolutionaries. As both sides came to the bargaining table, a coup was staged in Spain, in 1820 that changed the Spanish monarchy into a liberal institution; one that the central government in Mexico disfavored. The general placed in command to quell the revolutionary movements' military force and set the terms for their surrender; Augustín de Iturbide, was pushed into total defeat and opted instead to offer his own version of a truce. In reconciling both opposing sides on Jan 20, 1821, under the "Iguala" plan, also known as the "Three Guarantees" – the plan had three goals: establishing Mexico as a country with the Roman Catholic faith as its one religion; proclaiming Mexico as an independent nation; achieving social equality for every social and ethnic group within the country. That popularized it sufficiently with the revolutionary forces to give him the momentum to form an alliance with them. The "Trigaranté army" (Army of the Three Guarantees) was formed with the revolutionary armies and the government's troops under his own command, concluding the war for independence in Mexico. He signed "The Treaty of Córdoba" on August 24, 1821, with Don Juan O'Donnojú –a Spanish replacement meant to be the new viceroy assuring Mexico as an independent empire from Spain –its own constitutional monarchy recognized by the Spanish throne. In the treaty, Iturbide was decreed First Chief of the Imperial Mexican Army and on May 18, 1822, following his rousing, a popular movement named him Emperor Augustín I. On March 19, 1823 he abdicated power after his opponents had grown too numerous. They declared his disrespect of exercising power under the provisions of previous treaties and he was exiled, to Italy.

In 1824, he was executed after chasing the rumor of a possible Spanish invasion of Mexico. Guadalupe Victoria, an old revolutionary, was named the first president of Mexico, in 1824.

New Granada (northern South America) – In 1808 Venezuela proclaimed its Independence from Spain and sent Andrés Bello, Luis López Mendez, and Simón Bolívar to Great Britain on a diplomatic mission: a plan to foment full independence from Spain for all the colonies from the New World. On returning to Venezuela on June 3, 1811, he enlisted under the command of Francisco de Miranda who acted as dictator of Venezuela, fighting with him until he was defeated and imprisoned by royalist forces. Simón traveled to Cartagena and wrote the Cartagena manifesto: he argued for the cooperation of all the different kingdoms of New Granada. He was persuasive and successful and he continued leading the revolutionary cause, invading Venezuela, taking the city of Merida and the capital, Caracas. There he was proclaimed "el Libertador" (The Liberator). He was defeated by the Royalists, in 1814 and found asylum in Nueva Granada where he intervened and assisted in freeing Bogotá; after being appointed commander in chief of the forces of the federal republic. After falling out with province leaders, he sought refuge in Jamaica and there wrote the "Letter from Jamaica"; a document on the current struggle and purpose of Latinamerican independence. He returned to Venezuela, in 1817 with assistance from newly independent Haiti and continued fighting. On August 7, 1819, Bolívar defeated the Spanish at the battle of Boyacá and founded "la Gran Colombia" (The Great Colombia) at the Angostura congress; it represented the now present- day areas of Venezuela, Colombia, Panama, and Ecuador. He was named president. His military hand; Antonio José de Sucre, Francisco Antonio Zea, and Francisco Paula Santander, all kept fighting for a stronger and more independent state. Northern South America was completely liberated from all Spanish and royalist authority on May 22, 1822, when Antonio José de Sucre defeated the Spanish at Pichincha, in Ecuador. He began talks with the "Knight of the Andes," the liberator of southern South America, José de San Martín, to begin planning a total victory over the Spanish royalists. Eventually, he was made chief, and defeated the Spanish in the battle of Junin on August 6, 1824 and the battle of Ayacucho on December 9, 1824. Spanish rule over South America no longer existed. On August 6, 1825 the Republic of Bolivia was created at the congress of upper Peru, which had been invoked by Antonio José de Sucre.

Peru and "el Río de la Plata" (southern South America) – In 1810 a momentous French invasion of Spain allowed for the wealthy residents of Argentina to seize power; asserting their own authority under King Fernando VII, deposing the viceroy. On July 9, 1816, the Argentine Declaration of Independence was signed; the connecting ties to the Spanish monarchy began their eventual separation. In the north, remained the Royalist viceroy of Peru. Revolutionary movements, created to sever any possibility of Spanish rule were starting to formulate.

The splintered factions looking for personal gain which had earlier assumed authority were now in a position to claim complete control. José de San Martín, a lifelong soldier and veteran of the Napoleonic wars, offered his services, in 1812. In 1814, José de San Martín was appointed to command the Revolutionary Army. He later resigned and at the edge of the Chilean Andes and with the help of his longtime friend and Chilean patriot Bernard O'Higgins, enlisted support from the patriots residing in Chile and the Argentine government, raising an army: "el Ejército de los Andes" (The Army of the Andes). They crossed the Andes with success and defeated the Spanish on February 2, 1817: re-establishing a national government in Santiago, placing O'Higgins at the head as the Republic's first president, Chile was fully independent in April, 1818. After failing in negotiations with the Royalists, in Peru, upon Martin's suggestion that they themselves form an independent monarchy; Martín's forces began incursions into Peru and backed the remaining Spaniards into defeat, in 1821: the result of blocking their last remaining seaport. José de San Martín was proclaimed the protector of Peru. In 1822, he abdicated his powers at the first invocation of the Peruvian congress; he then left them in Bolívar's hand.

Cuba – Cuba remained loyal to Spain until 1868, when Carlos Manuel de Céspedes began the freedom movement with what was known as the "Grito de Yara" (Cry of Yara), to set Cuba free. This began a ten-year war waged by Cuban guerrillas known as the Mambises and they fought with victory and acclaim. As Cuba prepared for its independence, José Martí a famous poet and writer, started the Cuban Revolutionary Party. In 1878, the remaining revolutionaries in Cuba signed the pact of Zajón, providing general amnesty for all combatants and freeing all slaves involved in the act. Yet independence had not been reached and the United States had begun implementing its interests in expanding its reign over the small and treasured island. A small effort saw its initiation in Major Calixto García's and José Maceo's attempt at independence, called "la Guerra Chiquita" (The Little War). It was time for a renewed strategy. Calixto García, Antonio Maceo, Máximo Gómez, and José Martí banded together most of the veterans alive from the ten-year war and set sail from Florida to fight in Cuba. Combat led to a stalemate with the Spanish which the United States took advantage of, citing the precedent of the destruction of the U.S.S. Maine as a reason to engage Spain and annex Guam, Cuba, the Phillipines, and Puerto Rico from them. Martí died, in 1895 during an Invasion to Cuba. Cuba became a republic, in 1901.

Revolution

The development of Latin-American nations after their independence from Spain varied from country to country and was influenced by several factors that all held in common and that resulted in different stages and degrees of statehood.

Arriving at a stable position in government conflict between bilateral opposing parties (Liberal and Conservative) and reaching a peace with guerrilla movements or the democratically transforming, authoritarian, repressive regime has been the end-in-sight for most Latin-American nations in the 21st century. The mixture of the lower classes and ethnic Indian groups into the governmental structure, and the balance of foreign influence and encroachment were central causes for conflict and stagnation. Of those nations that did not sustain a democratic process, armed conflict between the government and its critical or armed opposition ensued in the form of armed and unarmed revolutionary movements, military coups, and state-sponsored military repression.

After independence, Mexico was involved in the Mexican-American war (1846-1848) with the United States during Antonio López Santa Anna's reign over the then unsettled state of Texas, which eventually became part of the United States. In 1855, Ignacio Comonfort bridged the gap between Liberals and Conservatives by becoming the nation's first moderate president. In 1857, the newly enacted constitution left the exclusivity of the Catholic Church as Mexico's sole religion unremarked and set off a bloody four year civil war that had liberals allying with moderates to stunt the conservatives' inclinations towards the Church's interest. The Liberals were the victorious ones, making Benito Júarez president. In the 1860's Mexico was invaded by France, who created the Second Mexican Empire, under Habsburg Archduke Ferdinand Maximilian of Austria. They were then overthrown by him and General Porfirio Díaz – the next president, aided by the United States. Their final victory on May 5, 1862, led by Ignacio Zaragosa, is the origination of the "Cinco de Mayo" celebrations. Porfirio Díaz inaugurated his presidency in 1876, through the Plan of Tuxtepec and remained in office for thirty years. His reign was called the "Porfiriato" because of its length and consistent production of public works aided by heavy foreign capital investment. The lower classes were systematically exploited and unrepresented in their motivations for social change. Francisco Madero intended to run against Díaz for the presidency in 1910 and was jailed by his opponent. He fled to the United States and initiated a revolt, with native Indians supporting him, which put him in power; through the support of other opposition leaders such as Zapata and Carranza and the United States. Disagreements over the issue of land reform with Zapata, who had written the "Plan de Ayala," led to the loss of popular support and instigated a coup d'etat by his military commander, Victoriano Huerta, who executed him and his vice-president one week later. Other leaders disagreed with his station and issuing the "Plan de Guadalupe," initiated a front-face conflict with him. Villa, Zapata, Carranza and Obregón fought him and forced him to flee to Puerto Mexico: the United States invaded Vera Cruz and these predicaments led him to flee to Spain. Carranza became the next president and was himself deposed by Villa and Zapata –the former who became president in 1915. Carranza adopted a new constitution, becoming president in 1917 and was again deposed, in 1920 by Obregón. Carranza was assassinated in 1920. He had assassinated Zapata in 1919. Villa was assassinated in 1923.

Obregon's successor Plutarco Elías Calles, assumed the presidency in all but in name in 1928, after his assassination. The Cristeros' rebellion: the Christian resistance to the government oppression of their faith predicated within the constitution of 1917, ended in 1929. The same year he created the National Revolutionary Party "PNR," that has had a nominee in every election held until 2001. In 1934, the progressive General Lázaro Cárdenas was elected president and in the following four decades coined the term "El Milagro Mexicano" (The Mexican Miracle), because of the nation's industrial rise and social advancement.

The Dominican Republic was occupied by Haiti for twenty-two years after their independence from Spain. They became free again in 1844 after Pedro Santana's military force expelled the invaders. He volunteered the Dominicans back into the Spanish Empire in 1861, and following a rebellion to this measure, the Domincans restored their independence, in 1865. The United States ruled the Dominican Republic, in 1916-1924, through a military government. The first elected president, in 1924, was Horacio Vásquez. In 1930, Rafael Trujillo, a prominent army commander ousted President Horacio Vásquez and established absolute political control as dictator. He modernized the nation through many public works, but his repressive regime fell hard upon any critics of its rule. He massacred twenty thousand Haitian sugar cane workers in a response to the Dominicans working in Haiti –across the border, to overthrow him. After trying to form a plan to assassinate the Venezuelan President Rómulo Betancourt, his government was singled out and acted against by the Organization of American States (OEA) and the United States. He was assassinated by his own troops. His son Ramfis Trujillo was president for a short while, but was then exiled as Joaquín Belaguer came into power. He resigned in 1962, and a council under President Rafael Bonnely held power, until 1963 when Juan Bosch of the "Partido Revolucionario Dominicano" (PRD or Dominican Revolutionary Party) was inaugurated president. He was overthrown by a right-wing military coup in 1963. A civilian triumvirate adopted a joint dictatorship, until 1965 when military elements vying for Bosch's return and the proponents of a new general election came to a head; anti-Bosche forces calling in the United States for assistance. In 1966 Balaguers' Reformers Party had him assume the presidency, and again in 1970, and 1974. In the 1978 election, he was defeated by Antonio Guzmán Fernández, marking the first peaceful transfer of power to an opposing party, in the nation's history.

After becoming a possession of the United States, the Republic of Cuba gained formal independence on May 20, 1902, with independent leader Tomás Estrada Palma becoming the country's first president. In 1906, a revolt in Cuba led to United States intervention –as was specified in their special amendments to the Cuban constitution. In 1908, José Miguel Gómez was elected president and power was transferred back to Cuban control. In 1925, Gerardo Machado y Morales suspended the constitution and made himself Cuba's first dictator. In 1933, a military coup deposed him and installed Carlos Manuel de Céspedes – not the same from the Cry of Yara, as Cuba's new leader.

TEACHER CERTIFICATION EXAM

Later that year, Sergeant Fulgencío Batista overthrew him and replaced him with Carlos Mendieta y Montefur. Aiming for Cuban sovereignty, Batista himself ran for president in 1940, but was opposed by the leader of the constitutional liberals Ramón Grau San Martín. He turned instead to the Communist Party of Cuba which eventually generated his election. Grau became president in 1944 and Carlos Prío Socarrás of the same party, in 1948. In 1952, he staged a coup –for he had slim chances of winning, and became dictator. In 1956, Fidel Castro and a group of young nationalists sailed to Cuba, on a boat called "Granma," –from Mexico, and began their insurrection in the Sierra Madre Mountains. Batista fled in 1959 and Fidel assumed power that has lasted to this day. In 1959, Osvaldo Dorticós Torrado became President as Fidel was the first secretary of the communist party. In 1976, a new constitution was introduced that made him President, while still remaining chairman of the council of ministers.

In 1838, Costa Rica proclaimed itself a sovereign and independent nation from its prior allegiance to "The United Provinces of Central America": consisting of the areas of Guatemala, El Salvador, Honduras and Nicaragua –under the rule of Braulio Carrillo. In 1856, William Walker, a United States explorer bent on conquering Central America and claming it to be part of the United States, invaded Costa Rica. He was repelled by the national army. In 1899, the first democratic elections were held under peacefull auspices. In 1917, Federico Torinco Granados ruled as dictator and was ousted, in 1919. In 1948, José Figueres Ferrer led an armed uprising to challenge the recent and questionable elections. In 1949, he abolished the army after two thousand casualties came out from a fourty-four day civil war.

Rafael Carrera was the leader who broke Guatemala away from "The United Provinces of Central America." He ruled until 1865. Starting in 1871, as president, Justo Rufino Barrios was the leader of the country's trend in modernization and also fought to reunite the Central American provinces. He was killed on the battlefield wanting to achieve this, in 1885. Manuel José Estrada came into power in 1898 and invited the United Fruit Company to do business with the country. A coup d'etat in 1920, installed General José Orellana into the presidency. In 1931, Jorge Ubico was unanimously elected president: a member of the Progressive party –he recognized himself as dictator. In 1944, his office was overthrown by the "October Revolutionaries," lead by Jacobo Arbenz and Francisco Javier Arana. A general election chose Juan José Arévalo as president, in 1945. In a failed coup Arana was killed, but Arbenz managed to succeed Arévalo in 1951, in a general election. The United States orchestrated a coup against his communist aligned government and Colonel Carlos Castillo Armas assumed power. He was assassinated in 1958 and General Ydígoras Fuentes assumed power. In 1960, a group of junior officers began their own rebellion which was stammered and led to their extending ties, with Cuba. In 1966, President Julio César Méndez Montenegro began counter-insurgency operations in the countryside.

FOREIGN LANGUAGE: SPANISH

The Guerrilla Army of the Poor (EGP), the Revolutionary Organization of Armed People (ORPA), the Rebel Armed Forces (FAR), and the Guatemalan Labor Party (PGT): all battled against the government and joined together as the Guatemalan National Revolutionary Unit (URNG), in 1982.
Right-wing groups The Secret Anti-Communist Army (ESA), The White Hand, battled the civilian population whom they identified as possible perpetrators and enemies. In 1982, junior officers willing to prevent the ascension of General Ángel Aníbal Guevara, as President, staged a coup d'etat. General Efraín Ríos Montt was elected. He promptly annulled the 1965 constitution, dissolved Congress, suspended political parties and cancelled the electoral law. He began forming local civilian defense patrols (PACs) and the resulting imbroglio constituted a mass genocide of the rural and Indian population. He was deposed, in 1983 by General Óscar Humberto Mejía Victores, whom allowed a return to democracy and a new constitution to be drafted, in 1985.

Honduran Francisco Morazán became the president of "The United Central American Provinces," in 1830 and upon its dissolution in 1838, intended to reunite them through force. He was ousted by General Francisco Ferrera who became President in 1841. Morazán was executed in 1842, in Costa Rica. United States soldier of fortune William Walker intended to invade, but was captured by the British and executed in Honduras, in 1860. Internal conflict between liberals and conservatives was swayed by the influence of like-minded-parties in neighboring Guatemala, El Salvador and Nicaraua. The United Fruit Company shipped its first shipment of bananas from Honduras and so became its center of exploitation. In 1899, the peaceful transfer of power from Liberal Policarpo Bonilla to General Sierra marked the first constitutional shift in power. After him Manuel Bonilla assumed power and set the foundation for the "Partido Nacional de Honduras" (National Party of Honduras or PNH) – which exists to this day. In 1956, a coup d'etat led by the former president's son ousted Lozano Díaz - then current President. The military dissolved congress in 1963 and assumed power. Suazo Córdova was the first civilian elected President in ten years in 1981.

In 1823, El Salvadorian Manuel José Arce formed "The United Central American Provinces." In 1832, Anastasio Aquino led an indigenous revolt against criollos and mestizos. In 1838, El Salvador became independent after "The United Central American Provinces" dissolved. General Maximiliano Hérnandez Martínez came into power during a coup, in 1931 and embraced a brutal oppression of all resistance movements: Farabundo Martí's peasant uprising, in 1932 was decimated into "La Matanza" (The Massacre). The National Conciliation Party held power from the early 1960s until 1979. In 1967, Fidel Sánchez Hernández became President and manned the helm during the brief "Soccer War" against Honduras. In 1972, José Napoleón Duarte, opposing military rule, ran for President and lost. An ensuing coup d'etat to impose his own rule led to his exile. Leftist guerrilla groups began to form and total war erupted in both the cities and the countryside.

Right-wing death squads began to kill indiscriminately: the Salvadorian Armed forces perpetrated the "El Mozote" massacre. In 1979, the Revolutionary Government Junta, a group of military officers and civilian leaders, ousted the President's and General Carlos Humberto Romero's right-wing government. In 1980, the murder of Archbishop Óscar Arnulfo Romero, whom had asked for the United States to stop granting aid to El Salvador's armed forces, led to a new constituent assembly. Álvaro Alfredo Magaña Borja was selected its provisional president. In 1980 all left-wing guerrilla groups coalesced into the Farabundi Martí National Front (FMNL). After drafting a new constitution, in 1983 Duarte was elected President, in 1984. In 1989, the Nationalist Republican Alliance's (ARENA) Alfredo Cristiani became president and marked the first time a switch within political power, between opposing sides, occurred without violence. After FMNL led an attack on the capitol San Salvador, in 1989 the FMNL and the government were invited to Peace talks with the UN, eventually leading to the Chapultepec Peace accord, and a cease-fire in 1992.

Nicaragua separated from "The United Central American Provinces," in 1838. In 1853, Conservative General Fruto Chamorro took over the government and exiled the liberals who previously held it in control. A civil war ensued. William Walker assumed power later, in 1856. In 1857, a constituent assembly convened and named General Martínez, as president. A revolt, in 1893, ousted Roberto Sacasa. General José Santos Zelaya, the man who initiated the revolt, was eventually called to be President. In 1926, General Emiliano Chamorro forced previous president Carlos Sólorzano from power. The "Ejército Defensor de la Soberanía de Nicaragua" (Army for the Defense of Nicaraguan Sovereignty), under Augusto César Sandino; fought against social inequality. Anastasio "Tacho" Somoza García established a military dictatorship, in 1937, after assassinating Sandino –whilst in negotiations about the possibility of a peace accord. Leonardo Argüelo was named President, in 1947 and then replaced, through Somoza's handywork, by Benjamín Lacayo Sacasa. Somoza was assassinated, in 1956 and was proceded by his son. The "Frente Sandinista de Liberación Nacional" (Sandinista National Liberaton Front), a student activist group, was created in 1961. In 1972, a three-man junta ruled the government. Following a Sandinista revolution, Dictator Anastasio Somoza Debayle was deposed and they took control of the government, in 1979. The United States granted aid to former National Guard members –organized and called "contrarevolucionarios" (counterrevolutionaries or contras), starting 1981. Daniel Ortega was sworn in as President, representing the new government, in 1985.

Panama seceded from Colombia in 1903 with support from the United States, brought on by the upper circles' desire to govern, indepently. Liberal and Conservative parties were organized and arrayed to govern. A revolutionary junta controlled the government. In a 1969 coup d'etat, General Omar Torrijos assumed power. He died in a plane crash in 1981. General Manuel Norriega assumed governmental control.

He annulled the elections, in 1989, that elected Guillermo Endara to power. Norriega was overthrown by the United States and left Endara in control.

In 1830, "La Gran Colombia" (The Republic of Greater Colombia) broke away into separate states: Venezuela, Quito (now known as Ecuador) and "Nueva Granada" (New Granada – is now Colombia and Panama), in which Bolívar became President. In 1850, "el Partido Liberal" (The Liberal Party or PL) and "el Partido Conservativo" (The Conservative Party or PC) were created and a Federalist-Nationalist friction was set into being. In 1853, the elected liberal president was deposed in a coup d'etat by General José María Melo, who dissolved congress and named himself dictator in 1854. His term lasted for eight months and was followed by conservative rule. In 1857, PC candidate Mariano Rodriguez adopted a new constitution and renamed the country the "La Confederación Granadina" (Grenadine Confederation). In 1861, conservative president Bartolomé Calvo was deposed by liberals led by General Mosquera. He drafted the constitution of Ríonegro in 1863, lasting until 1886. He renamed the country "The United States of Colombia." Mosquera was ousted and exiled in 1867. The federalist trends within the previous constitution were remade into a centrally organized political system, in the new constitution of 1886, put into place by nationalist opposition candidate Rafael Nuñez. Disenchanted liberals began "La Guerra de los Mil Días" (The Thousand Day War) with the Conservative government. They eventually signed a peace agreement, in 1902. Panama seceded from the country, in 1903. General Rafael Reyes became President, in 1904. He replaced Congress with a National Assembly. In 1930, Liberals took charge of the government through their first elected President in many years, Enrique Olaya Herrera. The current reformist policy encountered resistance and in 1946, the PL's candidate, who differed with previous policy, spurred Gaitán – a popular reformist, into running independently. In 1948, he was murdered –over an unrelated incident, and riots ensued throughout the capital destroying much of its downtown area –in an incident called "El Bogotazo." "La Violencia" (The Violence), a period of undeclared war between liberals and conservatives, claiming two hundred thousand lives over the next ten years followed. Congress was closed in 1949 by Mariano Ospina, and General Rojas Pinilla assumed power through a coup d'etat, in 1954. An alternating system of government was set in place called "El Frente Nacional" (The National Front). One term would be assumed by a Conservative candidate and the next one by a Liberal candidate. Alberto Lleras Camargo was the first president –a liberal, elected on the basis of the previous accord. Durign this period any opposition to the current agreement had no outlet in government and various guerrilla groups formed: "Ejército de Liberación Nacional" (National Liberation Army or ELN), "Fuerzas Armadas Revolucionarias Colombianas" (Armed Colombian Revolutionary Forces or FARC), "Ejército Popular de Liberación" (Popular Liberation Army or EPL) – these were all based in communist ideology. In 1974, the National Front ended and Alfonso López Michelsen became President, in a peacefull change of power.

Venezuela separated from "La Gran Colombia" (Republic of Great Colombia), in 1830. General Páez was elected, under the new 1830 constitution. In 1846, Páez selected Liberal General José Tadeo Monangas as his successor; and was exiled alongsideh every other conservative in the country. In 1858, almost all local caudillos (local leaders) were involved in "La Guerra Federal" (Federal War). General Juan C. Falcón was elected president after the war's termination. Antonio Guzmán Blanco established a Dictatorship, in 1870 centralizing the government. Later, in 1945, a coup d'etat placed Rómulo Betancourt in power which led to constituent assembly elections, in 1946. The elected President in 1948, Rómulo Gallegos, was overthrown by the military and along with prior coup leaders, sent into exile. A three-man military junta was put in control of government, and the 1936 traditionalist constitution replaced the recent 1947 draft. Dictator Pérez Jiménez was forced to abdicate in 1958. A five-man provisionary military junta was formed, and invoked a general election, in 1959. Rómulo Betancourt was elected president. The "Fuerzas Armadas de Liberación Nacional" (Armed Forces of National Liberation or FALN) surfaced in the 1960s, as a left-wing opposition group. Raúl Leoni proved in 1964, to be the first Venezuelan democratically elected leader to receive previous office while remaining at peace.

Independent Peru's first President was Simón Bolívar. General Andrés Santa Cruz y Calahumana marched into Peru and imposed a Peru-Bolivia confederation, in 1839. General Marshal Ramón Castilla assumed power, in 1845. In 1872, the first elected civilian President came to power, Manuel Pardo – leader of the "Partido Civilista" (Civilian Party or PC). General Andrés Avelina Cáceres assumed power, being elected President, in 1886. José Nicólas de Piérola overthrew him through the "Revolución de 1895" (1895 Revolution), and assumed power. Colonel Oscar Raimundo Benavides seized governmental power, in 1914. Augusto B. Leguía y Salcedo assumed the presidency through a preemptive coup d'etat, in 1919. He was overthrown, in 1932, by the military and died in prison. The "Alianza Popular Revolucionaria Americana" (American Popular Revolutionary Alliance or APRA) founded in Mexico, in 1924, was brought by Haya de la Torre into Peru. In 1931, Sánchez Cerro was elected President, beating APRAs' Haya de la Torre. He was assassinated, in 1993. The military overthrew the government, in 1948. They installed General Manuel A. Odría as President; the "Partido Demócrata Cristiano" (Christian Democratic Party or PDC) and "Acción Popular" (Popular Action or AP), were newly created democratic organs. Haya de la Torre returned from exile, in 1962, and upon winning the elections, was ousted by the military led by General Ricardo Pérez Gódoy, who held a provisional junta for one year. Fernando Belaúnde, a member of the PDC, was President after the junta re-convened elections, in 1963. General Vásquez Alvarado overthrew the government, in 1968. Elections were held, in 1978, for a constituent assembly and the drafting of a new constitution. Former President Belaúnde was re-elected, in 1980.

Guerrilla group "Sendero Luminoso" (Luminous Path or SL) was spawned, in 1980, by philosophy professor Abimáel Guzmán Reynoso and the "Movimiento Revolucionario Túpac Amaru" (Túpac Amaru Revolutionary Movement or MRTA), was created in Lima. Bernardo O'Higgins was Chile's first President after independence from Spain. The "Partido Liberal" (Liberal Party or PL), "Partido Conservador" (Conservative Party or PC) and "Partido Nacional" (National Party or PN) –were created in 1857. Congress led a revolt against President José Manuel Balmaceda Fernández, in 1891, and assumed power. He later commited suicide in Argentina. President Alessandri Dipalma was deposed by the military, in 1924, and then reinstated by supporters led by Carlos Ibáñez del Campo and Marmaduke Grove Vallejo, in 1925. The "Frente de Acción Popular" (Popular Action Front or FRAP) socialist party was spawned, in 1958. In 1973, leftist UP (Popular Union or Union Popular) president Salvadore Allende was either murdered or commited suicide after his government was ousted in a military coup d'etat, led by General Augusto Pinochet Ugarte, who established a dictatorship. Chileans elected Christian Democrat Patricio Ailwyn as interim President, in 1989.

Bernardino Rivadavia was the first president of the Republic of Argentina within the "Provincias Unidas de el Río de la Plata" (The United Provinces of the River Plate), in 1826. General Juan Manuel de Rosas established a Dictatorship, in 1835. Rosas was overthrown by General Justo José de Urquiza, who called a constituent assembly and promulgated a constitution, in 1853. In 1930, General José F. Uriburu ousted President Hipolito Irigoyen. President Ramon S. Castillo was overthrown, in 1944 by army colonels, led by General Juan Peron. He was victorious in the 1946 election and established a dictatorship. The "Revolución Libertadora" (Liberating Revolution) ousted him, in 1955, and placed an interim government in power, under General Eduardo Lonardi. He was deposed, and General Pedro Aramburu assumed power, in 1955. General Juan Carlos Onganía was deposed in 1970, and General Roberto M. Levingston was made President. Peron, returning from exile, in 1973, was elected President and died one year later. His wife María Isabel Peron, the vice president, assumed power. In 1976, she was deposed by the "Proceso de Reorganización Nacional," a military junta, under the leadership of Jorge Rafael Videla. In 1983, Raúl Alfonsín was elected President.

Ecuador separated from "La Gran Colombia" (Republic of Great Colombia), in 1830. Gabriel García Moreno unified the country under the Roman Catholic Church, in 1865. He was assassinated in 1875. In 1895, the "Partido Liberal Radical" (Radical Liberal Party) came to power, and reduced the power of the clergy ushering in a liberal plutocracy. In 1941, an Amazonian border dispute with Peru led to a war which Peru won, annexing two hundred thousand kilometers of its territory. In 1972, a nationalist military regime, seized power. In 1979, Ecuador returned to constitutional democratic rule, under President Róldos.

Spain

Spain is agriculturally diverse. In the north, wood and fish are plentiful. In the central region, wheat and similar grains are harvested. The south is the birthplace of famous wines and olive oils; rice, the famous Valencia oranges, lemons, dates, and other tropical fruits can be found in the southeast. The machinery, motor vehicle, and foodstuff industries are an important source of revenue. Spain is the eighth largest economy in the world.

Spain is temperate, although affected by various physical differences. The northern coast and mountainous region to the northwest are the coldest and has the most rainfall in the country. The south is warm. The central and southeast regions experience extreme climates: high temperature and dry heat in the summer and intense cold in the winter.

Administratively, Spain, including its possessions is divided into 15 regions; the north, which consists of Galicia, Asturias, Cantabria, El País Vasco, Navarra and La Ríoja; the central region, which consists of Castilla, Madrid and Extremadura; the south, which consists of Andalucía; the east, which consists of Cataluña, Valencia, Murcía and Aragón. Each region is unique in its traditions, culture, and in some cases its language. It would behoove the individual studying Spanish to research these in greater detail.

Major Cities

Madrid is the capital of and largest city in Spain. It has many places of historical interest like "el Museo del Prado," where one can find an impressive collection of works by great Spanish painters like El Greco, Velázquez and Goya; "el Palacio Real," one of the biggest and most luxurious palaces in the world; "el Parque del Buen Retiro," former recreational area for Spanish nobles; "la Puerta de Sol," the center of all Spain's highways.

Barcelona is the capital of Cataluña and Spain's principal seaport. The city is divided into two parts by "Las Ramblas," one of the most beautiful avenues in all of Europe. Barcelona has always been considered Spain's big artistic and cultural center.

Sevilla is the main city in Andalucía. The Cathedral of Sevilla is the largest gothic cathedral in the world and there one can find the tomb of Christopher Columbus.

Valencia is a port city on the edge of the Mediterranean and a large agricultural, industrial and commercial center.

Granada is situated at the foot of the Sierra Nevada. It was the Moor's last Spanish fort. El Albaicín is a place of interest because it is one of the largest tipsy villages in existence.

La Alhambra, immortalized by Washington Irving in his book by the same name and "el Generalife", another Moorish castle famous for its gardens are two other places of interest.

Córdoba was the governing capital of the Muslim empire and the most important cultural center in Europe in the tenth and eleventh centuries.

Toledo is located on the edge of the Tajo River. It was the residence of Spanish kings until 1560.

Cadíz is the Atlantic seaport.

Bilbao is the capital of Vizcaya and the industrial mining center of the north. Burgos is the former capital of Castilla and León. There one can find the tomb of "el Cid Campeador," Spain's first national hero.

Santiago de Compostela is a city in Galicia visited annually by thousands of religious pilgrims. Legend has it that the tomb of the apostle Santiago, patron saint of Spain, can be found there.

Salamanca is the site of one of the oldest European universities, the University of Salamanca, founded in the thirteenth century.

Mexico and Central America

Mexico is a rising industrial power in Latinamerica that has established industries in the fields of telecommunication, natural gas distribution, electric generation, and seaport and railroad construction. Its agricultural output mainly consists of the production of corn, beans, cotton and, potatoes. It is the world's major producer of silver which produces close to one quarter of the total revenue of the economy. It is one of the world's leading producers of natural gas and petroleum: it has the seventh largest oil reserve in the world.

Its capital, Mexico City, was founded by Hernán Cortes on the ruins of Tenochtitlan, former Aztec capital in 1521. It has many points of interest. Among these: "el Paseo de la Reforma" (the most elegant avenue in the capital), "el Zócalo" (the major square), "el Palacio de Bellas Artes" (the largest theater in the country; which also contains a huge Mexican art collection), "el Museo de Antropología," "la Cuidad Universitaria," "la Basílica de Guadalupe" patron saint of Mexico, "la Catedral," "Templo Mayo" (important ruins), the floating gardens on Xochimilco and the pyramids and temples of Teotihuacán.

Other important cities: Guadalajara (prinicipal center of agriculture and cattle raising), Veracruz and Tampico (important ports on the Gulf of Mexico), Acapulco and Puerto Vallarta (famous beaches), Taxco (national monument of architecture and industrial center of silver) and Chichen Itza (ruins of former Mayan city).

Mexico is considered geographically, to be part of North America. It is the northernmost and westernmost country in Latin America. Its central region, which is the most densely populated in the whole country, is a great plateau that opens up to the north into dry and hot desert areas. The east and west feature two mountain ranges: the Sierra Madre Occidental and the Sierra Madre Oriental which are outwardly surrounded by oceanfront facing lowlands. To the south, forest and tropical rainforest areas make up the land. The Tropic of Cancer divides the country into Tropical zones to the south and temperate zones to the north. Its northern border with the United States along the Río Bravo, or Río Grande, is the longest border in the world. The Isthmus of Tehuantepec is the southernmost point of North America and the northernmost point of Central America. It is the most populous Spanish speaking country in the world.

Guatemala's hot tropical climate permits for farming of various types of agricultural products. Its principal products are coffee, bananas, and sugar. In the north are lowlands and in the south is a costal area where the majority of the population resides, the rest of the country being mountainous. Mayan languages are prominent in rural areas. Its capital is Guatemala City.

Honduras is historically an agriculturally producing country producing sugar, bananas, and coffee; it recently has found a burgeoning textile and shrimp industry as a new source of revenue. The ruins of Copan are a point of interest for once being the center of Mayan civilization. Eighty percent of Honduras consists of mountains with plains along its costal area, lowland jungles in the northeast, and a valley in the northwest which is its most heavily populated area. The Negro River is its boundary with Nicaragua. Its capital is Tegucigalpa.

El Salvador has the second strongest economy in Central America with a thriving telecommunications, banking, and textile industry. Coffee is its main agricultural product, but it also produces cotton, and sugar cane. In El Salvador rest the Mayan ruins of Tazumal, Chalchuapa, and San Andrés. It is the only Central American country without a coastline to the Caribbean Sea.
Two mountain ranges cross El Salvador from east to west: the Sierra Madre on the north and the southern range that is made up by volcanoes. It has a central plateau that consists of rolling plains resting between both mountain ranges that serve as the land for the majority of the country's population. There are narrow plains on its coastline with the Pacific. The Lempa River emptying into the Pacific Ocean is its only navigable river. El Salvador is the smallest country in Central America. It is known offhand "el pulgarcito de las Américas," (Ameica's little thumb). Its capital is San Salvador. Nahuatl, an ancient Native American language is prominent in all parts of El Salvador.

Nicaragua is mainly an agricultural country producing corn, cotton, coffee, bananas, and tobacco. It is the largest cattle raising country in Central America. It contains seven percent of the world's bio-diversity. It is the largest country in Central America.

It has mountains in the north central region and lowlands adjoining the Atlantic and Pacific. One fourth of the country is protected as a natural park or biological reserve. The Masaya Volcanic national park is a point of interest. Its capital is Managua.

Costa Rica's chief products for exportation are coffee, and bananas. It also produces cocoa, sugar cane, potatoes, and many types of fruit. Recently the fields of pharmaceuticals, electronics, financial outsourcing, and software development have become main economic sources. Costa Rica is one of the oldest democracies in the Western Hemisphere. It is the only one that does not have an army. A civil guard maintains order. Costa Rica is home to five percent of the world's bio-diversity. The Corcovado and Tortuguero national parks and the Monterey cloud forest are points of interest. Its capital is San José. Costa Rica is the only country in Central America whose population consists mostly of Caucasian people. Spanish is the first and most common language but English is spoken often.

Panama's principal agricultural product is bananas, but the main source of its economy is banking and commerce. Its Colón free trade zone is the largest free trade zone in the Western Hemisphere. Panama is the smallest populated Spanish-speaking country in the Américas. It is considered a land bridge between South and Central America. The Isthmus of Panama is the dividing point where Central America ends and South America begins. Cristóbal is the terminus of the Canal Zone. Balboa is the port on the Pacific side. Its capital is Panama City. Panama is a melting pot; nine percent of its population is Chinese.

The Antilles (group of islands in the Caribbean Sea)

Cuba is the number one producer of sugar cane in the world. Cattle raising and fishing are also important industries and the country is rich in mineral deposits. It also produces tobacco – known worldwide for its quality, nickel, rice, and a large variety of fruits. Its organic agriculture initiative is noted for its innovation and the pharmaceutical industry is being heavily invested in.

Cuba's healthcare system, with free universal health care for all its people, is ranked as being one of the best in the world. Cuba is the largest island in the Caribbean and the last surviving communist state in Latinamerica. Cuba was the first of the Antilles to be discovered by Columbus on his first trip to the New World. It is known as the Pearl of the Antilles because of its beautiful country sides and fertile land. Its capital is Havana. The Castle of "el Morro" is a place of great historical interest because it was a fort used to protect the island from pirates in the seventeenth century. Guantanamo is an American naval base located on the island.

The Dominican Republic's economy is based on agriculture. Its main products are sugar cane, cocoa, coffee, plantains, and corn.

Citrus, green vegetables, pineapples, and flowers have grown important. Fishing is also becoming a major industry. It also bears the world's largest open-pit gold mine. It has three mountain ranges: the central, septentrional, and eastern that cut the island from east to west. In the south where most of the population concentrates are rolling plains, while the west is arid and is made up of shrubs and cacti. The north side of the island is made up mostly of beaches. The Dominican Republic occupies two-thirds of the island of Hispañola. The other third is occupied by Creole speaking Haiti. Lake Enriquillo is the lowest point in the Caribbean. Its capital is Santo Domingo. There one can find the first chapel, first hospital, and first cathedral in the New World, as well the oldest university in the New World: Thomas Aquinas University ,known today as the University of Santo Domingo.

Puerto Rico's main staple is sugar cane. The petrochemical, pharmaceutical, and technology industries are a rising addition to the current economy. It is mostly a mountainous island with coastlines on its north and south faces. The "Cordillera Central," the central mountain range, runs through the island. To the northwest lie beautiful beaches such as Jobos beach, María's beach, Domes beach and Sandy beach. The island came into posession of the United States, in 1898. Today it is known as a commonwealth. Its inhabitants have United States citizenship (since 1917). The island was discovered by Columbus, in 1493. The largest telescope in the world, the Arrecibo observatory, is situated on the island. Its capital San Juan, was established in 1508, by Ponce de León. It is an active commercial port and possesses beautiful and ancient forts from the Spanish Colonial era.

South America

Argentina has a traditional, middle class economy that is largely self-sufficient. Livestock and grains are the country's major source of revenue. Its economy's famed products, its wines and meats, are recognized to be excellent by the rest of the world. Textiles, leather goods, and chemicals are prominent products within the overall economy. It is the second largest country in South America and the seventh largest in the world. The "Tierra del Fuego" (Land of Fire) and Patagonia in the south are made up of grassland and thorny forests.

The Chaco, in the north and northeast, is made up of jungles, swamps, mountains; the Iguazu falls lie within it. The Pampas, the country's central fertile plains, are home to the majority of the country's population and agricultural industry. Buenos Aires its capital, possesses one of the most active seaports in the world. It is a very sophisticated city with a triage of elegant avenues, stores and theatres. Its second most important city is Rosario, a port city and industrial center. German, Spanish, and Italian immigrants make up most of the population with native Indians representing a small percentage of the total race makeup. It has the largest Jewish population in all Latinamerica. Uruguay's principal industry is cattle raising.

It is also one of the world's leaders in the production of cotton. Tobacco and sugar are agricultural staples. Textiles, soy beans, cement, and lime are produced as well. Vegetable oils are a rising industry. It is the smallest Spanish-speaking country in South America. It is made up of rolling plains and hundred of miles of beautiful beaches along the coast. El Negro River bisects the country from east to west. Montevideo is its capital and major port.

Paraguay's economy is agriculturally based. Its most important products are tea leaves, and wood. It is landlocked on both sides, east and west; but it has many navigable outlets to the River Plate estuary bordering the Atlantic. The Paraguay River cuts the country into two east-west sections. In eastern Paraguay between the Parana and Paraguay rivers, is the country's largest concentration of people. The west is mostly made up of marshes, lagoons, dense forests, and jungles. Its capital is Asunción and is also its major port. Guaraní is its other dominant language, besides Spanish.

Chile is the world's largest producer of copper and mineral ore. Its chief products are grapevines and cereals. It is the world's longest country. The southernmost point of South America Cape Horn; Punta Arenas, the southernmost urban area in the world; Easter Island, home to a mysterious ancient civilization; Patagonia, the polar south region adjoining Antarctica, are all points of interest. The central valley's rolling plains are home to the majority of the country's population and agricultural industry. The north region is the Atacama Desert, known as the driest place on earth. Its most important cities: Santiago, the capital; Valparaíso, the principal seaport; and Viña del Mar, a famous beach.

Bolivia has very rich mineral reserves that produce tin, copper, zinc, lead, sulfur, and gold. It has the second largest natural gas industry in South America. It is a landlocked country that only has access to the Atlantic through the Paraguay River. Bolivia's population is concentrated on the western part: a great plateau called the "Altiplano," where half its population lives. East are grasslands and rainforests. Lake Titicaca, located between Bolivia and Peru, is the tallest commercially navigable lake in the world and South America's largest freshwater lake. Within the department of Potosi lie the "Salar de Uyuni," the world's largest salt flats. The country is named after Simón Bolívar.

Its capital is La Paz: the capital with the tallest altitude in the world. Bolivia has the highest indigenous population ratio in all America. Spanish, Quechua, and Aymara are all equally recognized in Bolivia.

Peru's mining industry producing copper, gold, and other precious minerals for a major source of its revenue. It has widespread agricultural sectors, with a variety of products for both domestic and foreign markets such as corn, cotton, and different fruit trees. Fishing has always been a popular industry. In the north coast llamas, sheep, and goat-like animals are kept. Cebu cattle roam, fit to the Amazonian climate.

The Andes mountain ranges divide the country into three regions: the Pacific coast, which is desert-like; the sierra, which is dominated by the Andes and where more than half the country's population lies; the jungles of the Amazon, which cover more than sixty percent of the country. The Sechura dessert is located in the northwestern area close to the Pacific coastline. The roots of the Amazon River are located in Peru. Peru is home to eighty-four of the one hundred and four remaining ecosystems on earth. The Manu National Park is the most diverse rainforest in the world. The mysterious Nazca lines are found within the coastal plains. Near the city of Cuzco one can find the ruins of Machu Picchu, a former Incan city. There one can also find the University of San Marco, the first university on the continent; founded in 1551. Lima is its capital: an agricultural and industrial center, originally a fishing village. The city of Arequipe "la Ciudad Blanca" (The White City), is protected by UNESCO and is Peru's second largest city. Quechua is Peru's second official language.

Ecuador's main agricultural product is bananas, but petroleum is the economy's mainline. It also produces coffee, cacao, fine woods, flowers, shrimp, and tuna. It has a complete range of geographical features that include islands, mountains, beaches, and jungles. Most of the country's population is concentrated in the Pacific coast and in the central Andean sierra region. Cotopaxi south of Quito, is the world's tallest active volcano. The Galápagos Islands; the site of Charles Darwin's inspiration for the "Theory of Evolution," are a point of interest. Quito is Ecuador's capital and Guayaquil is its main port city. Cuenca is the center for the most part, of all the artisans who produce pottery, silver plates, and gold work within the country.

Colombia main products for exportation are: coffee –which it is world-famous for, topsoil, bananas, and petroleum. It is the United States' largest exporter of flowers. It also produces carbon, gold, silver, platinum, and emeralds. The Andes mountain range separates the country from the southeastern Ecuatorial border to the northwestern Venezuelan border. It separates into three mountain ranges, the "Cordillera Oriental," the east mountain range; the "Cordillera Central," the central mountain range; the "Cordillera Occidental," the west mountain range; all at the Colombian Massif. The Magdalena River runs to the coast and starts where the eastern and central mountain ranges separate; it is its principal river. East of the eastern mountain range are "llanos," extense grasslands.

The Cauca River, which separates the central and western mountain ranges into a fertile valley, is the second largest river and one of the Magdalena's main affluents. The plateau in its central region and its extending basins are the country's most populated areas. There are lowlands west of the western mountain range and in the north by the Caribbean coastline. The south is made up mostly of jungle and dense forest. Colombia is one of the most bio-diverse countries in the world. "Parque Tayrona" (Tayrona National Park), is a point of interest conjoining beaches, mountains and mountain forests.

Bogotá is its capital and Medellín is its second most important city -it is the industrial nexus of coffee production and one of the fastest growing economic regions in South America. Cartagena is its principal commercial seaport and within it one can find intact colonial artifacts and architecture. It has many points of interest like: "la Ciudad Vieja" (The Old City,) the old colonial city with colonial houses and churches; "La Muralla" (The Old wall), a wall surrounding the city, bridled with cannons, that was utilized to protect it from English pirates; "El Castillo San Felipe" (San Felipe's Castle), a large castle built for the same purposes.

Venezuela produces coffee and cocoa. However, the agricultural industry is minimal: petroleum is the base of its economy. It has the world's seventh largest oil reserve. The northeastern extension of the Andes mountain range lies in the country's northwest region. Its population is concentrated in the mountainous regions of the east and in its coastal regions. The central region is made up of "llano," savannah and extends to the banks of the Orinoco, its main river and border with Colombia. The south called the Guiana Highlands, is featured by mountain forests and jungles. Lake Maracaibo is the largest body of water in northern Venezuela and if considered a lake - it is connected to the Caribbean Sea by a fifty-four mile strait - it is the largest body of water in South America. The world's tallest waterfall "Salto Ángel" (Angel Falls), lies in the south. The "Cuevas de Guacharo" (Guacharo Caves) are Venezuela's largest and most magnificent caves. Caracas is both the political and commercial capital of the country. It is a modern city with beautiful streets and buildings.

In 1826, Simón Bolívar made the first attempt to bring world leaders together. He invited representatives from all the nations of the New World to come together in Panamá. Though only four countries sent delegates, the Panama Conference was still a success. The First International Conference was held in the United States (Washington, D.C.) in 1889 – 1890. Its purpose was to maintain peace and better commercial relations between countries. In the Conference of Buenos Aires in 1920, the Panamerican Union was created. Its purpose was to establish cultural and economic ties between 21 nations.

In 1948, the ninth Panamerican Conference took place in Bogotá. The alliance was recognized and given a new name "Organización de Estados Americanos - OEA" (organization of American States). It is now part of the United Nations and has many functions.

Some of these functions are: to maintain peace among its members, to mutually assist each other in times of need and to work towards cultural, social and economic progress.

The "Área de Libre Comercio de las Américas," (Free trade Area of the Americas), a United States initiative to reduce trade barriers, was initiated with NAFTA (North American Free Trade Agreement) with Mexico, in 1994.
It eventually aims to enact multiple TLCs' "Tratados de Libre Comercio," (Free Trade Agreements) with every nation in the American continent, except Cuba.

SUBAREA V—WRITTEN EXPRESSION

0014 Use Spanish to present in writing information, concepts, and ideas for a variety of purposes to different audiences.

Complete the following exercises and answer the following referring to the written material in section 0005.

- Compose an oral discourse that recreates the experience of eating at the "Maki Roll."

SUBAREA VI—ORAL EXPRESSION

0015 In response to a prompt, effectively communicate an oral message in Spanish that includes a range of vocabulary, idiomatic expressions, complex language structures, and sociolinguistic appropriateness.

Complete the following exercises and answer the following referring to the written material in section 0005.

- What do you think about Chavez's threat to expel the U.S ambassador in Venezuela? Write a short essay to defend your opinion.

Selected Bibliography

The American Heritage Spanish Dictionary (1986). Boston: Houghton Mifflin.

Diccionario de la Lengua Española (2003) 23rd ed. Madrid: Real Academia Española

Diccionario Manual VOX Illustrado de la lengua Española Nueva Edición (1996). Barcelona: Espasa-Calpe

Blair, Rober W. (ed.) (1982). *Innovative Approaches to Language Teaching.* Massachusets: Newbery House.

Cantarino, Vicente (1986). *Civilizaciòn y cutura de España* (2nd ed.) New Jersey: Prentice Hall.

Chan-Rodriquez, Raquel, and Filer, Malva E. (1988). *Voces de hispanoamèrica: antologia literaria.* Boston: Heinle & Heinle.

Garcìa, Carme and Spinelli, Emily. (1995). *Mejor dicho.* Massachusetts: D.C. Heath.

Gill, Mary McVey, Wegmann, B., and Mèndez-Faith, T. (1995). *Encontacto: lecturas intermedias* (5th ed.) New York: Harcourt Brace.

Guntermann, Gail (ed.) (1993). *Developing Language Teachers for a Changing World.* Illinois: National Textbook Company.

Hashemipur, Peggy, Maldonado, R., and Van Naerssen, M. (eds.) (1995). *Studies in Language Learning and Spanish Linguistics.* New York: McGraw-Hill.

Keen, Benjamin (1992). *A History of Latin America* (4th ed). Boston: Houghton Mifflin.

Liskin-Gasparro, Judith (1987. *Testing & Teaching for Oral Proficiency.* Boston: Heinle & Heinle.

Marin, Diego, and del Rìo, Angel. (1966). *Breve historia de la literature española.* New York: Holt, Rinehart and Winston.

Marquès, Sarah. (1992). *La lengua que heredamos: curso de español para Bilingües.* (2nd ed.) New York: John Wilery & Sons.

Omaggio Hadley, Alice (1993). *Teaching language in context.* (2nd ed.) Goston: Heinle & Heinle.

Rojas, Jorge Nelson & Curry, Richard A. (1995). *Gramàmatica esencial: repaso y pràctica.* Boston: Houghton Mifflin.

Samaniego, Fabiàn A., Alarcòn, F.X., Rojas, N., & Gorman, S.E. (1995). *Mundo 21.* Massachusetts: D.C. Heath.

Spinelli, Emily, Garcia, C., & Galvin, C.E. (1994). *Interacciones.* (2nd ed.). Florida: Holt, Rinehart, and Winston.

REGULAR VERB CONJUGATIONS

VIVIR

Commands (Imperative) live
Informal: vive tú; no vivas
Formal: viva Ud.; vivan Uds.

Present Indicative	Preterite Indicative	Imperfect Indicative	Present Progressive	Present Subjunctive
Live/lives/living	*lived*	*lived/used to live*	*am/are/is*	*live*
do (does) live	*did live*	*was(were) living*	*living*	*may live*
vivo	viví	vivía	estoy	viva
vives	viviste	vivías	estás	vivas
vive	vivió	vivía	está + viviendo	viva
vivimos	vivimos	vivíamos	estamos	vivamos
vivís	vivisteis	viviáis	estáis	viváis
viven	vivieron	vivían	están	vivan

Imperfect Subjunctive	Past Progressive	Present Perfect Indicative	Pluperfect Indicative	Future Indicative
lived	*was/were +*	*have/has*	*had*	*will*
might live	*living*	*lived*	*lived*	*live*
viviera	estaba	he	había	viviré
vivieras	estabas	has	habías	vivirás
viviera	estaba + viviendo	ha + vivido	había + vivido	vivirá
viviéramos	estábamos	hemos	habíamos	viviremos
vivierais	estábais	habéis	habíais	viviréis
vivieran	estaban	han	habían	vivirán

Conditional Indicative	Present Perfect Subjunctive	Past Perfect Subjunctive	Future Perfect Indicative	Conditional Perfect Indicative
would	*may have*	*might have*	*will have*	*would have*
live	*lived*	*lived*	*lived*	*lived*
viviría	haya	hubiera	habré	habría
vivirías	hayas	hubieras	habrás	habrías
viviría	haya + vivido	hubiera + vivido	habrá + vivido	habría + vivido
viviríamos	hayamos	hubiéramos	habremos	habríamos
viviríais	hayáis	hubierais	habréis	habríais
vivirían	hayan	hubieran	habrán	habrían

COMER

Commands (Imperative) eat
Informal: come tú; no comas
Formal: coma Ud.; coman Uds.

Present Indicative	Preterite Indicative	Imperfect Indicative	Present Progressive	Present Subjunctive
eat/eats/eating	*ate*	*ate/used to eat*	*am/are/is*	*eat*
do (does) eat	*did eat*	*was(were) eating*	*eating*	*may eat*
como	comí	comía	estoy	coma
comes	comiste	comías	estás	comas
come	comió	comía	está + comiendo	Coma
comemos*	comimos	comíamos	estamos	comamos
coméis*	comisteis	comíais	estáis	comáis
comen	comieron	comían	están	coman

Imperfect Subjunctive	Past Progressive	Present Perfect Indicative	Pluperfect Indicative	Future Indicative
ate	*was/were +*	*have/has*	*Had*	*will*
might eat	*eating*	*eaten*	*eaten*	*eat*
comiera	estaba	he	Había	comeré
comieras	estabas	has	habías	comerás
comiera	estaba + comiendo	ha + comido	había + comido	comerás
comiéramos	estábamos	hemos	habíamos	comeremos
comierais	estábais	habéis	habíais	comeréis
comieran	estaban	han	habían	comerán

Conditional Indicative	Present Perfect Subjunctive	Past Perfect Subjunctive	Future Perfect Indicative	Conditional Perfect Indicative
Would	*may have*	*might have*	*will have*	*would have*
Eat	*eaten*	*eaten*	*eaten*	*eaten*
comería	haya	hubiera	habré	habría
comerías	hayas	hubieras	habrás	habrías
comería	haya + comido	hubiera + comido	habrá + comido	habría + comido
comeríamos	hayamos	hubiéramos	habremos	habríamos
comeríais	hayáis	hubierais	habréis	habríais
comerían	hayan	hubieran	habrán	habrían

*Note: -er and –ir verbs share the same verb endings except for the nosotros and vosotros forms in the present indicative:
   -er verbs end in –emos/-éis   -ir verbs end in –imos/ -ís

TEACHER CERTIFICATION EXAM

MIRAR

Commands (Imperative) look
Informal: mira tú; no mires
Formal: mire Ud.; miren Uds.

Present Indicative	Preterite Indicative	Imperfect Indicative	Present Progressive	Present Subjunctive
look/looks/looking	*looked*	*looked/used to look*	*am/are/is +*	*look*
do (does) look	*did look*	*was(were) looking*	*looking*	*may look*
miro	miré	miraba	estoy	mire
miras	miraste	mirabas	estás	mires
mira	miró	miraba	Está + mirando	mire
miramos	miramos	mirábamos	estamos	miremos
miráis	mirasteis	mirabais	estáis	miréis
miran	miraron	miraban	están	miren

Imperfect Subjunctive	Past Progressive	Present Perfect Indicative	Pluperfect Indicative	Future Indicative
looked	*was/were +*	*have/has*	*had*	*will*
might look	*looking*	*looked*	*looked*	*look*
mirara	estaba	He	había	miraré
miraras	estabas	has	habías	mirarás
mirara	estaba + mirando	ha + mirado	había + mirado	mirará
miráramos	estábamos	hemos	habíamos	mirariemos
miraráis	estábais	habéis	habíais	miraréis
miraran	estaban	han	habían	mirarán

Conditional Indicative	Present Perfect Subjunctive	Past Perfect Subjunctive	Future Perfect Indicative	Conditional Perfect Indicative
would	*may have*	*might have*	*will have*	*would have*
look	*looked*	*looked*	*looked*	*looked*
miraría	haya	hubiera	habré	habría
mirarías	hayas	hubieras	habrás	habrías
miraría	haya + mirado	hubiera + mirado	habrá + mirado	habría + mirado
miraríamos	hayamos	hubiéramos	habremos	habríamos
miraríais	hayáis	hubierais	habréis	habríais
mirarían	hayan	hubieran	habrán	habrían

Common Verbs with Irregular Forms in the Present Subjunctive

The present subjunctive is formed by first conjugating the infinitive in the first person in the present indicative. Always begin with the infinitive.

Examples:

Infinitive	First Person	Indicative	Subjunctive
Mirar	Yo	Miro	Mire
Comer	Yo	Como	Coma
Vivir	Yo	Vivo	Viva
Decir	Yo	Digo	Diga
Hacer	Yo	Hago	Haga

Infinitive	First Person	Indicative	Subjunctive
Poner	Yo	Pongo	Ponga
Pensar	Yo	Pienso	Piense
Contra	Yo	Cuento	Cuente
Servir	Yo	Sirvo	Sirva
Morir	Yo	Muero	Muera

Exceptions are the six Spanish verbs that do not end in –o in the first person singular:

Infinitive	First Person	Indicative	Subjunctive
Dar	Yo	Doy	Dé
Estar	Yo	Estoy	Este
Ser	Yo	Soy	Sea
Ir	Yo	Voy	Vaya
Saber	Yo	Sé	Sepa
Haber	Yo	He	Haya

Common Verbs with Irregular Forms in the First Person Singular

Present Indicative

Infinitive	Yo	Tú	Ud./él/ella	nosotros/as	vosotros/as	Uds./ellos/ellas
caber	quepo	cabes	cabe	cabemos	cabéis	caben
conocer	conozco	conoces	conoce	conocemos	conoceis	conocen
dar	doy	das	da	damos	dais	dan
hacer	hago	haces	hace	hacemos	hacéis	hacen
poner	pongo	pones	pone	ponemos	ponéis	ponen
saber	sé	sabes	sabe	sabemos	sabéis	saben
salir	salgo	sales	sale	salimos	salís	salen
traer	traigo	traes	trae	traemos	traéis	traen
valer	valgo	vales	vale	valemos	valéis	valen
ver	veo	ves	ve	vemos	veis	ven

Common Verbs with Irregular Forms in the Future and Conditional Indicative

The future and conditional tenses are formed by adding a series of endings to the entire infinitive or to a corrupted infinitive. The endings work for all verbs, no exceptions: -ar, -er, -ir.

Note the forms of the present perfect of haber:	Future Endings	Infinitive	Corrupted Infinitive	Conditional Endings
he	é	haber	habr-	ía
has	ás	poder	podr-	ías
ha	pa	querer	querr-	ía
hemos	emos	saber		íamos
habéis	éis			íais
han	án			ían
		venir	vendr-	
		poner	pondr-	
		salir	saldr-	
		tener	tendr-	
		valer	valdr-	
		decir	dir-	
		hacer	har-	

Common Verbs with Irregular Forms in the Preterite Indicative

Meaning	Infinitive	Yo	Tú	Ud./é/ella	Nosotros/as	Vosotros/as	Uds./ellos/ellas
to have	tener	tuve	tuviste	tuvo	tuvimos	tuvisteis	tuvieron
to be	estar	estuve	estuviste	estuvo	estuvimos	estuvisteis	estuvieron
to walk	andar	anduve	anduviste	anduvo	anduvimos	anduvisteis	anduvieron
to know	saber	supe	supiste	supo	supimos	supisteis	supieron
to put	poner	puse	pusiste	puso	pusimos	pusisteis	pusieron
to be able	poder	pude	pudiste	pudo	pudimos	pudisteis	pudieron
to want	querer	quise	quisite	quiso	quisimos	quisteis	quisieron
to do, make	hacer	hice	hiciste	hizo	hicimos	hicisteis	hicieron
to come	venir	vine	viviste	vino	vinimos	vinisteis	vinieron
to say, tell	decir	dije	dijiste	dijo	dijimos	dijisteis	dijeron
to bring	traer	traje	trajiste	trajo	trajimos	trajisteis	trajeron
to give	dar	dije	diste	dio	dimos	disteis	dieron
to see	ver	vine	viste	vio	vimos	visteis	vieron
to go	ir	fui	fuiste	fue	fuimos	fuisteis	fueron
to be	ser	fui	fuiste	fue	fuimos	fuisteis	fueron

FOREIGN LANGUAGE: SPANISH

Verbs Irregular in the Imperfect

There are only three irregular verbs in the imperfect.

Meaning	Infinitive	Yo	Tú	Ud./él/ella	Nosotros/as	Vosotros/as	Uds./ellos/ellas
to be	ser	era	eras	era	éramos	erais	eran
to go	ir	iba	ibas	iba	ibamos	ibais	iban
to see	ver	veía	veías	veía	veíamos	veíais	veían

Common Verbs with Irregular Past Participles

He		
Has	+	-ado
Ha	+	-ido
Hemos	+	-to
Habéis	+	-cho
Han		

Abrir	Abierto
Cubrir	Cubierto
Escribir	Escrito
Morir	Muerto
Poner	Puesto
Romper	Roto
Ver	Visto
Volver	Vuelto
Decir	Dicho
Hacer	Hecho

TEACHER CERTIFICATION EXAM

MAP OF SPAIN

TEACHER CERTIFICATION EXAM

MAP OF LATIN AMERICA

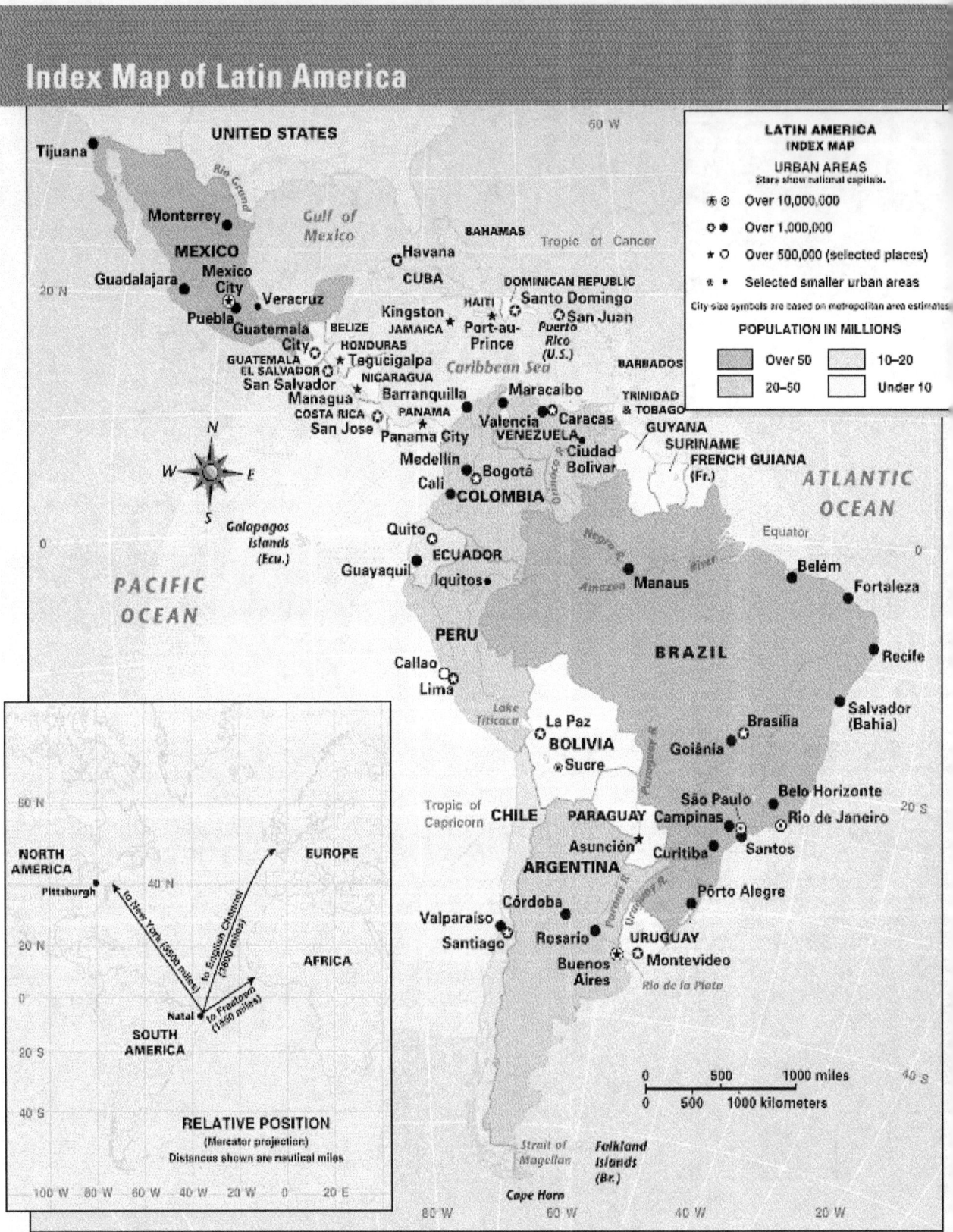

FOREIGN LANGUAGE: SPANISH

TEACHER CERTIFICATION EXAM

MAP OF THE CARIBBEAN

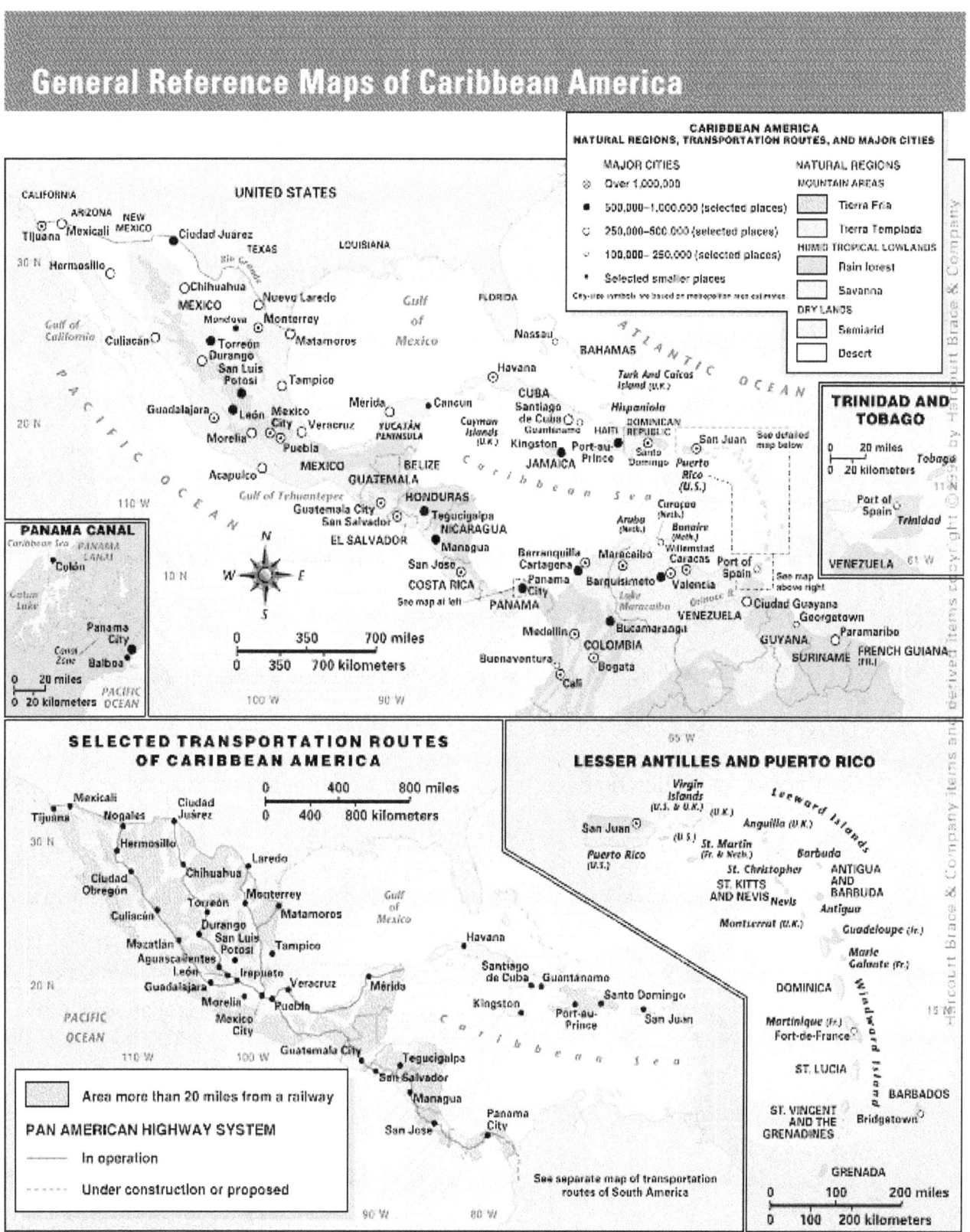

FOREIGN LANGUAGE: SPANISH

TEACHER CERTIFICATION EXAM

Practice Examination

I. Speaking Portion.

For this portion of the state exam you will be asked to record your answers in Spanish. Follow all directions on the cassette tape provided at the exam site.

Give the following directions in Spanish:

1. Take out your books. - Saquen sus libros.

2. Pick up your papers and books. – Recojan sus libros y sus papeles.

3. Write your answers on the blackboard. – Escriban sus respuestas en el tablero.

4. Please get into groups of four or five. – Por favor fórmense en grupos de cuatro o cinco.

5. Complete the following for homework. – Completen lo siguiente de tarea.

6. Hand in your homework. – Entrega tu tarea.

7. Describe where you went on your last vacation and what you did there. – Describe a donde fuiste en tus últimas vacaciones y lo que hiciste ahí.

8. Explain what sporting event(s) you plan to watch or attend this coming season: with whom, where, and why? – ¿Explica cuales eventos planeas ver o atender esta próxima temporada y con quién iras? ¿Dónde iras? ¿Porqué?

9. Narrate and explain how you spent your last major holiday. – Narra y explica como pasaste el último día festivo.

10. Describe how you will spend your next family celebration. – Describe como vas a pasar tu próxima celebración familiar.

11. Explain what your favorite book is and why. - ¿Explica tu libro favorito y porqué es?

12. Describe your favorite kind of music. - Describe tu música favorita.

13. What hobby would you like to pursue in more depth? Why? - ¿Qué pasatiempos te gustaría seguir con más profundidad? ¿Porqué?

14. Explain a news story you have been following in the paper or on the television. – Explica una historia de noticias que has leído en el periódico o en el noticiero.

15. Describe a political event or story of importance to you. – Describe un evento político o una historia política de importancia para ti.

16. Where do you live and why do you live there? - ¿Dónde vives y porqué vives ahí?

17. What advice would you like to give to the president about the importance of education funding in the 21st century? - ¿Qué consejo te gustaría dar al Presidente sobre la importancia del presupuesto educativo en el siglo veintiuno?

18. What do you think about efforts being done about the environment in your state and in the country in general? Why? - ¿Qué piensas sobre los esfuerzos que se hacen para el medio ambiente en tu estado y en el país en general?

19. What would you advise students about working long hours after school? Defend your opinion. - ¿Qué les aconsejarías a los estudiantes sobre trabajar muchas horas después del colegio? Defiende tu opinión.

20. Do you think professional athletes should be held to higher standards than other public figures? Why? – ¿Tú piensas que los deportistas profesionales deberían ser medidos por estándares más altos que los de otras figuras públicas? ¿Porqué?

TEACHER CERTIFICATION EXAM

II. Listening portion.

Please note a written script is provided in these sample materials. However, the state examination will not include a written text, written questions, and written choices in this segment of the test.

Listen carefully to the following passages and questions. Answer the following based upon what you heard. {*Audio script is in italics*}

21. ¿Cuál es el propósito de esta reunión?

Rigoberta Menchú, indígena Guatemalteca, nacida en 1959, ganó el Premio Nóbel de la Paz en 1992. Viajará a varios países, entre ellos, España. Menchú va a estar en Madrid donde dialogará con el nuevo Presidente del Gobierno Español sobre los problemas que sufre la población indígena de América Latina, a quien Rigoberta Menchú dedica sus esfuerzos y trabajo.

A. Viajar a varios países Europeos.

B. Ganar mucho dinero.

C. Recibir el Premio Nóbel de la Paz.

D. Ayudar a las personas menos afortunadas.

22. ¿Qué le gusta al Príncipe Felipe?

El Príncipe Felipe de Borbón, el futuro lider de España, nació en 1968. Estudió en Canadá y en los Estados Unidos. Es muy atlético y le interesa mucho los deportes. Lleva una vida bastante normal aunque es famoso. Está bien preparado para ser el próximo Rey de España segun las políticas Europeas.

A. Los norteamericanos.

B. Los canadienses.

C. Los deportes.

D. Los estudios.

FOREIGN LANGUAGE: SPANISH

TEACHER CERTIFICATION EXAM

23. ¿Cómo cambió mi estilo de vivir?

Antes de obtener mi licencia de conducir yo siempre tenía que depender de otras personas para ir a cualquier parte. No era independiente. No podia salir con mis amigos impulsivamente. Ahora tengo más libertad y independencia.

¿Cómo cambió mi estilo de vivir?

    A. Radicalmente.

    B. Impulsivamente.

    C. Solamente.

    D. Dependiente.

24. ¿Adónde van ellos primero?

Por favor. Mañana tienes que salir temprano conmigo para ir de compras porque voy a tener una fiesta el sábado. Espero que haya las tortillas en la Bodega García porque no tengo tiempo de ir al supermercado Solano en Miami. ¡Ojalá que yo tenga suficiente comida para todos los invitados!

¿Adónde van ellos primero?

    A. Una fiesta.

    B. Al supermercado

    C. A una bodega.

    D. A Miami.

25. ¿Qué deben comprar?

En la sala sólo hay un sillón de cuero y una lámpara; entonces necesitamos un sofá para sentarnos y una televisión para ver nuestros programas favoritos. En el comedor nos falta una mesa grande; aunque hay seis sillas.

¿Qué deben comprar?

    A. Un sillón de cuero y una lámpara.

    B. Un sofá, una televisión y una mesa grande.

    C. Una mesa grande y seis sillas.

    D. No nos falta nada.

III. Writing section: Choose the most accurately written item.

26. A. Es necesario que él estudiar.

    B. Es necesario que él estudié.

    C. Es necesario que él estudie.

    D. Es necesario que él estudia.

27. A. Necesito leer el libro.

    B. Necesito que yo leo el libro.

    C. Necesito que yo lea el libro.

    D. Necesito que yo leer el libro.

28. A. El lápiz de el es azul.

    B. Él lápiz de el es azul.

    C. El lápiz de él es azul.

    D. Él lápiz de él es azul.

29. A. Si tuviera el dinero viajara a Japón.

    B. Si tuviera el dinero viajará a Japón.

    C. Si tuviera el dinero viajaré a Japón.

    D. Si tuviera el dinero viajaría a Japón.

30. A. ¡Que pena que él se fuera!

    B. ¡Qué pena que él se fue!

    C. ¡Que pena qué él se fue!

    D. ¡Qué pena que él se fuera!

31. A. ¿Porque lo hiciste tú?

    B. ¿Por qué lo hiciste tú?

    C. ¿Por qué lo hiciste tu?

    D. ¿Porque lo hiciste tu?

32. A. El fumar es prohibido.

    B. Él fumar es prohibido.

    C. La fumar es prohibido.

    D. Fumando es prohibido.

33. A. Además de leer, me gusta nadando.

    B. Además de leyendo, me gusta nadando.

    C. Además de leer, me gusta nadar.

    D. Además de leyendo, me gusta nadar.

34. A. Nos gusta esquiar y navegar.

    B. Nos gustamos esquiar y navegar.

    C. Nos gusta esquiando y navegando.

    D. Nos gusta esquiar e navegar.

FOREIGN LANGUAGE: SPANISH

35. A. Se me olvidé la cartera.

B. Se me olvidó la cartera.

C. Me la olvidó la cartera.

D. Me la olvidé la cartera.

36. A. Cuando regresamos de México vamos a mostrarle las fotos.

B. Cuando regresemos de México vamos a mostrarle los fotos.

C. Cuando regresemos de México vamos a mostrarle las fotos.

D. Cuando regresamos de México vamos a mostrarle los fotos.

37. A. Los regalos son para tú.

B. Los regalos son para tu.

C. Los regalos son para ti.

D. Los regalos son para te.

38. A. En mí opinión, la gente es muy buena.

B. En mi opinión, la gente es muy buena.

C. En mi opinión, la gente son muy buena.

D. En mí opinión, la gente son muy buena.

39. A. ¿Viste a Mónica y a Carmen?

B. ¿Viste Mónica a Carmen?

C. ¿Viste a Mónica Carmen?

D. ¿Viste Mónica y Carmen?

40. A. Se puso la chaqueta por el frío.

B. Se puso la chaqueta para el frío.

C. Puso la chaqueta por el frío.

D. Puso la chaqueta para el frío.

Choose the correct response or most appropriate rejoinder:

41. ¿Quién lo hizo?

   A. –Yo lo hice.

   B. –Yo me hice.

   C. –Yo lo hizo.

   D. –Me lo hizo.

42. ¿Cuándo estudiaste para el examen?

   A. –Estudió anoche por dos horas.

   B. –Estudio anoche por dos horas.

   C. –Estudiaste anoche por dos horas.

   D. –Estudié anoche por dos horas.

43. Èl habla tres idiomas.

   A. –¡Que bien que habla tres idiomas!

   B. –¡Que bien que hable tres idiomas!

   C. –¡Que bien que hablo tres idiomas!

   D. –¡Que bien que hablas tres idiomas!

44. Me dolía la cabeza la semana pasada.

   A. –¿Fue al médico?

   B. –¿Fue el médico?

   C. –¿Iba el médico?

   D. –¿Fuiste el médico?

45. ¿Lo conoció en el colegio?

   A. –Sí, lo conoció allí.

   B. –Sí, me conocí allí.

   C. –Sí, lo conocí allí.

   D. –Sí, me lo conoció allí.

46. ¿Cuándo prepararás la comida?

   A. –La preparé mañana.

   B. –La prepararás mañana.

   C. –La prepara mañana.

   D. –La prepararé mañana.

47. Me importan los asuntos de lo que habíamos hablado.

   A. –A mi me importan tampoco.

   B. –A mi me importan también.

   C. –A mi me importan tambien.

   D. –A mí me importan tampoco.

FOREIGN LANGUAGE: SPANISH

Choose the rule or explanation that best explains the following:

48. **Esta mañana Lisette tomaba el sol y yo me bañaba en el mar.**

   A. Incorrect: The two verbs should be in the preterite because the actions occurred at a specific time.

   B. The subordinate verb should be in the preterite tense to contrast the two main events.

   C. The use of "bañarse" is not appropriate.

   D. The imperfect tense can be used to describe two or more actions going on at the same time in the past.

49. **Eran las 2:00 cuando salimos ayer por la tarde.**

   A. Correct: The imperfect tense is used to tell time in the past.

   B. Incorrect: Both verbs should be in the imperfect to describe past actions.

   C. Incorrect: The preterite tense is used to tell time in the past.

   D. Correct: Both verbs are in the imperfect tense to tell a story.

50. **Trabajamos para dos horas.**

   A. Correct: "Para" is used to indicate a deadline.

   B. Correct: "Para" is used to indicate a length of time.

   C. Incorrect: "Por" is used to indicate a specific hour.

   D. Incorrect: "Por" is used to indicate a length of time.

51. **Busco el estudiante que vendió el libro.**

   A. Incorrect: The subordinate verb should be in the subjunctive.

   B. Correct: The indicative is used to indicate a known or specific person.

   C. Personal "a" should form the contraction "al" when a person is the direct object.

   D. Correct: The object of the verb is not a specific person thus the personal "a" is not used here.

52. Estaban viendo la televisión cuando alguien tocó la puerta.

A. Incorrect: The imperfect tense is used to tell a story.

B. Incorrect: The imperfect tense is used to indicate past actions.

C. Correct: The imperfect tense is used to describe the past.

D. Correct: The imperfect tense sets the stage for another action to take place.

53. Quisiera que ella lo hiciera.

A. Correct: The imperfect subjunctive is used following the preterite.

B. Correct: The imperfect subjunctive is used following a past subjunctive.

C. Incorrect: The imperfect subjunctive is used to express doubt in the past.

D. Correct: The imperfect subjunctive is used to express emotion in the past.

54. Música es el idioma universal.

A. Incorrect: The definite article is needed with nouns to point out a specific person or thing and is used with nouns expressing an abstract or generalized concept.

B. Incorrect: The word "idioma" is feminine.

C. Correct: The word "música" is too general a concept to be labeled "la música."

D. Correct: The verb "ser" is used to define.

55. Señora Cabrices es de Caracas, Venezuela.

A. Correct: The verb "ser" is used to express origin or nationality.

B. Correct: The preposition "a" is not needed.

C. Incorrect: The verb "estar" is used to express location.

D. Incorrect: The definite article should precede a title of someone's name.

56. **Mis hermanos y yo somos altas.**

   A. Correct: The verb "ser" is used to describe physical attributes.

   B. Correct: The compound subject requires the verb "somos."

   C. Correct: The possessive pronoun should be in the plural form.

   D. Incorrect: The plural adjective should be in the masculine plural form.

57. **¿Quién es? –Será la niñera.**

   A. Incorrect: The future tense is not used to respond to a question in the present.

   B. Correct: The future tense is used to indicate probability.

   C. Correct: The subject is understood.

   D. Incorrect: The subject should precede the verb.

58. **La problema prinicipal es que no han hecho nada.**

   A. Correct: Most nouns ending in "-ma" are feminine.

   B. Incorrect: Most nouns ending in "-ma" are masculine.

   C. Correct: The word "no" precedes the present perfect construction.

   D. Correct: Spanish requires the double negative.

59. **Mi padre es pesimista pero mi madre es optimista.**

   A. Incorrect: Adjectives should agree in both gender and number wiht the noun they modify.

   B. Incorrect: The conjunction "sino" should be used in the negative construction.

   C. Correct: The subjunctive mood is not needed to express an opinion.

   D. Correct: Adjectives that end in "ista" have only one singular form for masculine and feminine nouns.

TEACHER CERTIFICATION EXAM

60. Si irás conmigo, será mejor.

   A. Incorrect: The future tense is never used in the "si" clause.

   B. Correct: The future tense is alwyas used in the "si" clause.

   C. Correct: The future tense is used to express probability.

   D. Correct: The "si" clause denotes more of a probability than a possibility.

61. ¿Saben ustedes cómo tocar el piano?

   A. Incorrect: "Como" used in a question requires a written accent mark.

   B. Incorrect: "Saber" is used to indicate the knowledge of a fact.

   C. Incorrect: "Saber" when used to indicate knowledge of how to do something does not require the word "como."

   D. Correct: "Tocar" is used to mean play a musical instrument and "jugar" is used to mean to play a sport or game.

62. Quiero que él lo haga.

   A. Correct: Object pronouns are attached to affirmative direct commands.

   B. Correct: Object pronouns precede a conjugated verb in both the indicative and subjunctive moods.

   C. Incorrect: The present subjunctive is formed by dropping the "-o" of the first person singular present indicative of regular verbs.

   D. Incorrect: The subjunctive is used to express an implied command.

63. Se venden muchos autos aquí.

   A. Correct: "Se" is used to express an unknown plural subject "they."

   B. Correct: The verb is plural to agree with the plural object.

   C. Incorrect: "Se" is used to denote a reflexive action.

   D. Incorrect: "Se" is only used with the third person singular form of the verb, not the plural.

FOREIGN LANGUAGE: SPANISH

TEACHER CERTIFICATION EXAM

64. Mi abuela está muerta.

A. Correct: "Estar" expresses a condition as the result of something.

B. Correct: "Ser" should be used here to designate a permanent condition.

C. Incorrect: "Estar" is used to denote a temporary state.

D. Incorrect: "Muerto" is the past participle of "morir."

65. No lo han leído.

A. Incorrect: The object pronoun precedes the past participle.

B. Incorrect: The past participle should be plural to agree in number with the subject.

C. Incorrect: The past participle does not require a written accent mark.

D. Correct: The object pronoun precedes the entire verb phase.

66. ¿Qué es esto?

A. Correct: "Esto" is neuter demonstrative pronoun and does not take a written accent mark.

B. Correct: When demonstrative adjectives replace a noun they are called demonstrative pronouns.

C. Incorrect: "Esto" requires a written accent mark.

D. Incorrect: Demonstrative pronouns are used to point out.

67. Vendimos nuestra antigua casa hace muchos años.

A. Incorrect: Only quantitative adjectives can precede a noun.

B. Incorrect: Only qualitative adjectives can precede a noun.

C. Correct: The meaning of "antigua" in this context is to denote the former home.

D. Correct: The meaning of "antigua" is this context is to denote the very, very, old home.

FOREIGN LANGUAGE: SPANISH

68. Tampoco voy a la biblioteca.

   A. Correct: The negative word can precede the verb.

   B. Incorrect: The negative can never precede the verb.

   C. Correct: The antecedent of the subordinate clause is conveyed through the context of the dialogue.

   D. Incorrect: Spanish requires the use a double negative.

69. Se comió el pollo Raúl.

   A. Incorrect: The subject should precede the object of the sentence.

   B. Correct: The verb agrees with the subject of the sentence.

   C. Incorrect: The verb "comer" is not reflexive.

   D. Correct: The verb is in the singular to agree with the object of the sentence.

70. Èl es un buen estudiante.

   A. Incorrect: The qualitative adjective should not precede the noun.

   B. Correct: The verb "estar" implies a temporary quality or condition.

   C. Incorrect: The indefinite article is not used with an occupation.

   D. Correct: The adjective "bueno" is shortened before a singular masculine noun.

71. Se me perdieron los libros.

   A. Correct: The "me" is used here as an indirect object pronoun.

   B. Incorrect: The ver should agree in number with the subject of the sentence.

   C. Correct: The "me" is used here as a reflexive pronoun.

   D. Incorrect: The word "se" is not needed with the verb "perder."

72. Anoche estuve enfermo.

A. Incorrect: The preterite describes a specific action or event in the past.

B. Correct: The imperfect describes an emotional activity in the past.

C. Correct: The preterite can be used to emphasize that an action has ended.

D. Incorrect: The imperfect expresses a temporary condition in the past.

73. Ayer iba al cine cuando vino Diego.

A. Correct: The imperfect describes a past repetitive action.

B. Correct: The imperfect stresses an action in progress when another action took place.

C. Incorrect: The preterite is needed to express a past fact.

D. Incorrect: The preterite expresses an action that took place at a definite time in the past.

74. Ella es mayor que yo.

A. Correct: Implies she is physically bigger than I am.

B. Correct: Implies she is older than I am.

C. Incorrect: Implies she is the oldest of all.

D. Incorrect: Implies she is greater than I am.

75. Hay más que veinte personas.

A. Correct: The comparative requires a written accent.

B. Incorrect: When this comparison is followed by a number the form is "mas de."

C. Correct: The numeral 20 requires "mas de" but not the written form of the number.

D. Incorrect: The correct comparative is "mayor" for greater than.

76. Por favor, René. El carro está sucio. Lávalo.

A. Incorrect: The command form is not needed here. It is a request.

B. Incorrect: The object pronoun should precede the conjugated verb.

C. Correct: The affirmative command is in the familiar form.

D. Correct: The negative familiar command has the same form as the second person singular.

77. Isabel me conocía por primera vez en 1992.

A. Correct: The verb "conocer" denotes knowing a person.

B. Correct: The verb "saber" denotes factual knowledge.

C. Correct: The imperfect of "conocer" implies met for the first time.

D. Incorrect: The preterite of "conocer" implies met for the first time.

78. El agua es pura.

A. Correct: The word "agua" is masculine.

B. Correct: "El" is used although the word "agua" is feminine.

C. Incorrect: The word "agua" is not masculine.

D. Incorrect: The word "agua" is feminine and it should be "La."

79. Ella me preguntó dinero.

A. Correct: "Preguntar" is used to ask a question.

B. Correct: "Preguntar" is used to request something.

C. Incorrect: "Pedir" is used to request something.

D. Correct: "Preguntar" is used to ask for something or to inquire.

80. Necesito el informe para el lunes.

A. Incorrect: "Para" is used to express a length of time.

B. Correct: "Por" is used to express a length of time or specific hour.

C. Incorrect: "Por" is used to indicate a specific deadline.

D. Correct: "Para" is used to indicate a specific deadline.

81. ¿Qué es la capital de Colombia?

   A. Correct: ¨Qué¨ is used to ask for a definition.

   B. Correct: ¨Qué¨ is used to elicit a choice between two or more items.

   C. Correct: ¨Qué¨ is used to elicit a choice.

   D. Incorrect: ¨Cuál¨ is used to imply a choice in the response.

82. Los médicos trabajan para el hospital.

   A. Correct: ¨Para¨ is used to indicate employed by.

   B. Incorrect: ¨Para¨ is used to designate the recipient of an action or destination.

   C. Incorrect: ¨Por¨ is used to indicate employed by.

   D. Incorrect: ¨Por¨ is used to express occupations.

83. No hay algún restaurante por aquí.

   A. Incorrect: Spanish often requires a mulitple negative construction.

   B. Incorrect: The negative word ¨no¨ is used to precede the verb.

   C. Correct: ¨No¨ precedes the verb.

   D. Correct: ¨Alguno¨ is shortened to ¨algún¨ before a masculine singular noun.

Choose the appropriate answer to complete the following items:

84. José Martí (1853-1895), es de ___.

A. México.

B. Chile.

C. Cuba.

D. Argentina.

85. En 1971 Pablo Neruda (1904-1973) recibió el Premio Nóbel de ___.

A. Literatura.

B. Arte.

C. Ciencía.

D. la Paz.

86. Machu Picchu en el Perú es la antigua ciudad sagrada de los ___.

A. Mayas.

B. Incas.

C. Aztecas.

D. Olmecas.

87. Se celebra el Día de los Reyes Magos en ___.

A. noviembre.

B. diciembre.

C. enero.

D. febrero.

88. Nicaragua está situada entre ___.

A. Honduras y Costa Rica.

B. Costa Rica y Panamá.

C. Guatemala y El Salvador.

D. Guatemala y Belice.

89. El deporte de jai alai es de origen ___.

A. Catalán.

B. Árabe.

C. Griego.

D. Vasco.

TEACHER CERTIFICATION EXAM

90. **Sor Juana Inés de la Cruz (1651- 1695) era ___ mexicana.**

    A. Una artista.

    B. Una muralista.

    C. Una poeta y ensayista.

    D. Una novelista.

91. **El ¨Guernica¨ es el título de ___.**

    A. Un poema.

    B. Una pintura.

    C. Un drama.

    D. Una novela.

92. **___ ocurrió 1936-1939.**

    A. La Primera Guerra Mundial.

    B. La Segunda Guerra Mundial.

    C. La Revolución dé la Independencia Estaunidense.

    D. La Guerra Civil Española.

93. **El ¨TLC¨ refiere al ___.**
    A. Tratado comercial entre los EEUU, Canadá y México.

    B. Tratado del 16 de septiembre.

    C. Tratado de Guadalupe Hidalgo.

    D. Tratado Liberal Cubano.

94. **Tenochtitlán era la capital de los ___.**

    A. Aztecas.
    B. Mayas.

    C. Zapotecas.

    D. Incas.

95. **Frida Kahlo era ___.**

    A. Una novelista mexicana.

    B. Una fotógrafa moderna.

    C. Pintora mexicana del período surrealista.

    D. Una Patriota mexicana.

96. **Rigoberta Menchú es activista social de ___.**

    A. Guatemala.

    B. Cuba.

    C. Colombia.

    D. México.

97. **El autor de ¨Cien años de soledad¨ es ___.**

    A. Salvador Allende.

    B. Gabríel García Márquez.

    C. Miguel de Cervantes.

    D. Carlos Fuentes.

98. ___ es cantante de ópera, nacido en México, de padres Españoles.

   A. Diego Rivera.

   B. Julio Iglesias.

   C. Luis Miguel.

   D. Plácido Domingo.

99. El gran artista "El Greco," nació en ___.

   A. Grecia.

   B. Galicia.

   C. Italia.

   D. Toledo.

100. Andalucía, Cataluña, Galicia y Extremadura son ___.

   A. Ciudades españolas.

   B. Ciudades latinoamericanas.

   C. Provincias españolas.

   D. Provincias latinoamericanas.

101. La "sobremesa" es la costumbre de ___.

   A. Poner la mesa antes de comer.

   B. Limpiar la mesa después de comer.

   C. Charlar antes de comer.

   D. Charlar después de comer.

102. Al recibir una invitación a cenar, usted debe preguntar ..

   A. ¿Qué va a servir?

   B. ¿A qué hora debo llegar?

   C. ¿Qué debo comer?

   D. ¿Qué debo llevar?

103. Se celebra la Nochebuena el ___.

   A. 24 de diciembre.

   B. 25 de diciembre.

   C. 31 de diciembre.

   D. 6 de enero.

104. Por lo general en lo países latinoamericanos, se usa el tuteo para hablar con ___.

   A. Profesores y agentes de policía.

   B. Abogados, médicos y enfermeros.

   C. Amigos y miembros de la familia.

   D. Negociantes y empleados en tiendas.

105. Los curanderos recetan remedios naturales ___.

A. Porqué todos prefieren curarse en casa.

B. Porqué no hay recursos médicos modernos.

C. En algunos pueblos pequeños de España y América Latina.

D. En todos los hospitales y centros importantes de investigación científica.

106. Se puede regatear en ___.

A. Bodegas pequeñas.

B. Restaurantes.

C. Mercados de pulgas.

D. Almacenes en pueblos pequeños.

107. La típica familia española es ___.

A. Más grande en la actualidad que la del pasado.

B. Más pequeña en la actualidad que la del pasado.

C. Muy grande hoy en día.

D. Muy pequeña hoy en día.

108. Al ver el nombre "María Dolores Santamaría García" sabemos que ___.

A. Ella es casada.

B. Él nombre maternal dé ella es Dolores.

C. Él nombre maternal dé ella es Santamaría.

D. Él nombre maternal dé ella es García.

109. Se usa pronombre "vos" en ___.

A. España.

B. Lecturas y discursos.

C. Argentina, Perú, Chile, Ecuador y en otros países.

D. Antiguas obras literarias.

110. Termine el dicho: "Dime con quién andas y ___."

A. Déjala correr.

B. Mona se queda.

C. Se lo pondra.

D. Te diré quién eres.

Complete the following statements about foreign language teaching methodology:

111. The theory that input is easier to understand, produce, and recall when it is motivated and episodically organized most accurately explains ___.

A. Communicative methodology.

B. The purpose of role-playing activities.

C. Krashen's theory of Input + 1.

D. Oller's Episode Hypothesis.

112. Conversation cards and interviews are ___.

E. One type of oral achievement testing.

F. Functions of a language.

G. Language proficiency.

H. Examples of acquistions vs. Learning.

113. Proficiency guidelines are ___.

A. For describing and measuring language competence.

B. Theories of language teaching.

C. Methods for language acquisition.

D. Strategies for teaching language.

114. An achievement test measures ___.

A. Form vs. Function.

B. A student's general progress and ability.

C. A student's ability to comprehend written and spoken language.

D. A student's acquisition of specific knowledge of the course material.

Choose the item which best describes the following:

    A. Grammar-Translation Method
    B. Audiolingual Method
    C. Natural Approach
    D. Total Physical Response

115. Language is a set of habits, requiring oral practice of pattern drills and memorized responses. _____

116. The emphasis is on communicative competence rather than memorizing grammar rules and stressing accuracy. _____

117. This was originally used to teach Greek and Latin. Students learn elaborate grammar rules and bilingual lists of words. _____

118. This makes use of oral commands; students demonstrate their comprehension by physically reacting to the content of the message. _____

IV. Reading Comprehension. Read the short passages below and then choose the most accurate response based on your reading:

FEDERICO GARCÍA LORCA

El famoso poeta español Federico García Lorca fue asesinado durante la Guerra Civil Española. Fue uno de los miembros más distinguidos de la llamada generación del 27. Su muerte fue trágica para el mundo entero.

García Lorca nació en Fuente Vaqueros en Granada el 5 de junio de 1898. Cuando era joven asisitió en "la Facultad de Filosofía y Letras" en la ciudad de Córdoba. Pero un poco después fue a Madrid para seguir sus estudios. Allí conoció a Pablo Picasso, Salvador Dalí, Manuel de Falla y Andrés Segovia. Durante su vida tuvo la oportunidad de pintar, tocar la guitarra, escribir y viajar a Argentina, Cuba y los Estados Unidos.

Desafortunadamente murió entre circumstancias misteriosas el 19 de agosto del año 1936, pero su espíritu y talento viven hoy en día en su poesía y sus obras de teatro. Su muerte fue una profunda pérdida.

119. García Lorca asistió a universidades en ___.

A. Córdoba y Madrid.

B. Granada, Córdoba y Madrid.

C. Granada y Córdoba.

D. Argentina, Cuba, y los Estados Unidos.

120. Se hizo amigo de Picasso, Dalí, de Falla y Segovia en ___.

A. Granada.

B. Córdoba.

C. Fuente Vaqueros.

D. Madrid.

121. La idea principal de este pasaje es que García Lorca ___.

A. Viajó mucho.

B. Murió muy jovencito.

C. Fue un escritor con mucho talento.

D. Tenía muchos amigos.

122. Cuando murió, García Lorca tenía ___.

A. 27 años.
B. 36 años.
C. 38 años.
D. 49 años.

TEACHER CERTIFICATION EXAM

LA TRAVIESA TORMENTA

Hoy por la mañana, los investigadores del Centro Urbano predijeron que la tormenta se alejaría de la costa aunque cientos de miles de habitantes hubieran huido de las playas e islas costeras, causando un frenético embrollo. Esta tarde, su trayectoria sigue alejándose de la región. La tormenta tenía más de 200 millas de ancho y vientos de 110 millas por hora.

123. ¿Todavía hay una amenaza por la costa?

    A. Si, hay un frenético embrollo.

    B. Si, la tormenta es traviesa.

    C. No, las playas están lejanas.

    D. No, la tormenta se alejo de el área.

124. ¿De qué tipo evento meteorólogico trata la lectura?

    A. Un terremoto.

    B. Una llovizna.

    C. Un embrollo.

    D. Un huracán.

125. ¿Por qué huyó la gente?

    A. Para estar segura.

    B. Para ser vulnerable.

    C. Para volver a casa.

    D. Para ser traviesa.

TEACHER CERTIFICATION EXAM

Answer Key

1. – 20. varies	41. A	63. B	85. A	107. B
21. D	42. D	64. A	86. B	108. D
22. C	43. A	65. D	87. C	109. C
23. A	44. A	66. A	88. A	110. D
24. C	45. C	67. C	89. D	111. D
25. B	46. D	68. A	90. C	112. A
26. C	47. B	69. B	91. B	113. A
27. A	48. D	70. D	92. D	114. D
28. C	49. A	71. A	93. A	115. B
29. D	50. D	72. C	94. A	116. C
30. A	51. C	73. B	95. C	117. A
31. B	52. D	74. B	96. A	118. D
32. A	53. B	75. B	97. B	119. A
33. C	54. A	76. C	98. D	120. D
34. A	55. D	77. D	99. A	121. B
35. B	56. D	78. B	100. C	122. C
36. C	57. B	79. C	101. D	123. D
37. C	58. B	80. D	102. B	124. D
38. B	59. D	81. D	103. A	125. A
39. A	60. A	82. A	104. C	
40. A	61. C	83. A	105. C	
	62. B	84. C	106. C	

Go to xamonline.com for our latest product offerings including:
extra sample tests, flash cards, and expanded study guides.

www.ingramcontent.com/pod-product-compliance
Lightning Source LLC
Chambersburg PA
CBHW080542300426
44111CB00017B/2832